# The Balkan Women

## by Jules Tasca

A SAMUEL FRENCH ACTING EDITION

# SAMUEL FRENCH

FOUNDED 1830

NEW YORK HOLLYWOOD LONDON TORONTO

SAMUELFRENCH.COM

ISBN 978-0-573-69626-8          Printed in U.S.A.          #4917

## IMPORTANT BILLING AND CREDIT REQUIREMENTS

***THE BALKAN WOMEN*** had its world premiere at the Bristol Riverside Theater in Bristol, PA, in February 1998. The production was prodcued by Bristol Riverside Theater with the following cast:

LT. JOVAN VLACO . . . . . . . . . . . . . . . . . . . . . . . . . . . . . Sean Dougherty
SAMIRA JUSIC . . . . . . . . . . . . . . . . . . . . . . . . . . . . . Elizabeth Mestnik
AMINA JUSIC . . . . . . . . . . . . . . . . . . . . . . . . . . . . . . . . . . . . . Marta Vidal
JELA KALJANAO . . . . . . . . . . . . . . . . . . . . . . . . . . . . . . . . Maya Israel
COL. BRANISLAV HERAK . . . . . . . . . . . . . . . . . . . . Stephen Schnetzer

Winner of the 1997/1998 Barrymore Award for Best New Play

# CHARACTERS

**SAMIRA JUSIC** – A Muslim prisoner in a Serbian camp.

**AMINA JUSIC** – Samira's mother

**COLONEL BRANISLAV HERAK** – The camp Commandant

**LIEUTENANT JOVAN VLACO** – One of the camp interrogators.

**JELA KALJANAO** – Another Muslim prisoner

There is also a polyphonic chorus of four men and four women, adjuncts to the actors. The chorus sometimes speak with the characters to give emphasis, force or punctuation to a line.

*Dedicated to the famous*
*Nellie Tasca*

*(The set consists of two banks of stone steps upstage right and left. There is a wall of stone archways behind them with a chain link fence and barbed wire. Behind that wall is a walkway which can be accessed by going up either set of stone steps through two archways upstage right and left. A table a chairs will be brought on for Herak's cabin.)*

*(Beautiful folk music plays – possibly strings and a flute. We see women sitting on the steps on either side of the stage. Mothers sit and talk as they sew on a blanket and wash clothes in a bucket. On the other side of the stage, two younger women play a game and giggle. Another young woman joins them. It is SAMIRA, daughter of Amina. AMINA sees her and goes over to SAMIRA. She seems to be scolding her. The music pauses. Another young woman appears above. It is JELA – unseen by the women below. She plays on a flute more of the folk song. She stops. There is a very loud TICK – TICK – TICK. Silence. A LOUD EXPLOSION, perhaps a flash of light and smoke coming from behind the audience. The sounds of screams, sirens and soldiers marching also comes from behind the audience. The women on stage are frantic. The mothers gather the young women and begin to head inside. At that moment, soldiers march down the center aisle and onto the stage. They grab the women, forcing them up the stage left stone steps and through the corridor. They re-enter stage right, and one by one, the soldiers throw them onto the steps. A cell door slams as each woman is thrown in a cell. The soldiers march to the stage left bank of steps as one soldier, VLACO, emerges and addresses the audience.)*

**VLACO.** I'm Jovan Vlaco. I was a lieutenant in the Serbian army.

These women you see are Muslims, mother and daughter, Amina and Samira. We're here in what they call

**VLACO AND ALL WOMEN.** Southern Bosnia

**VLACO.** and we call

**VLACO AND ALL MEN.** Greater Serbia.

**VLACO.** All wars begin with the changing, of words and phrases.

**VLACO AND EVERYONE.** And this is war.

**VLACO.** They stand in the damp yard of our detention camp where the chill reaches past their clothes and skin and fingers their bones.

(**VLACO** *steps out of the light and crosses to the male chorus.* **AMINA** *and* **SAMIRA** *quicken. They rub their arms to warm themselves.*)

**SAMIRA.** What will they do to us?

**AMINA.** I don't think they'll do anything to us.

**SAMIRA.** How can you say that, mother?

**JELA.** You know what these

**JELA AND FEMALE CHORUS.** dirty dogs do to Muslim women.

**AMINA.** Quiet. Don't lose control of your wits.

(**JELA KALJANAO**, *a girl somewhat older than Samira, enters with a large bag. She sidles up to* **SAMIRA** *and* **AMINA**.)

**JELA.** God is great.

**AMINA.** God is great.

**JELA.** I'm Jela Kaljanao *(She offers them a roll from her bag.)* Take it then. Take it. I deliver the stale bread they give us. Eat whatever they give you.

**AMINA.** *(taking a roll)* Thank you.

**JELA.** *(as* **SAMIRA** *takes a roll)* I counted 125 when they, marched you women in. Hardly, any space in those cages, and you...

**SAMIRA.** Me? What?

**JELA.** I'd mess up your hair and hunch over.

**SAMIRA.** Why?

**JELA.** Don't make yourself look attractive.

**JELA.** The guards are all men. They don't need much incentive to

**JELA AND FEMALE CHORUS.** spread your thighs like a wish-bone.

**AMINA.** We'll be all right. We'll be all right, Samira.

**JELA.** I'm sorry you're in here, but it was glorious for who-ever blew up the fuel depot.

**AMINA AND FEMALE CHORUS.** It was frightening.

**JELA.** You know anything about it?

**AMINA AND FEMALE CHORUS.** What would we know?

**AMINA.** We don't know anything at all.

**JELA.** Hey, I'm one of you. If I knew who blew their depot. I'd

**JELA AND FEMALE CHORUS.** kiss her and praise her to Allah.

**AMINA.** We don't know anything.

**SAMIRA.** When will they let us go?

**JELA.** Who knows. I've been here for months. They question us over and over. They don't rush anything.
Except when they decide to

**JELA AND FEMALE CHORUS.** shoot one of us.

**JELA.** Then...then they move with

**JELA AND FEMALE CHORUS.** fire flying from their asses.

**JELA.** You hear the

**JELA AND FEMALE CHORUS.** pop

**JELA.** and one of us is gone.

**SAMIRA.** Who do they shoot?

**JELA.** You need names? They shoot us.

**JELA AND FEMALE CHORUS.** Us. Muslims. How they hate us. How the bastard Serbs hate us.

**JELA.** You think they hated you outside. In this place hate is the ground you stand on. Hate is...

*(as* **VLACO** *crosses into the scene)*

Here comes Vlaco.

**JELA AND FEMALE CHORUS.** Don't took him in the eye.

*(***JELA*** crosses away.)*

**VLACO.** Identification.

**AMINA.** *(handing him her papers from her dress)* I want to see the officer in charge of the camp. I want to tell him there's some mistake.

**VLACO.** The commandant's been reassigned. The new commandant arrives tomorrow.

**AMINA.** Then I want to see the new commandant.

**VLACO AND MALE CHORUS.** I don't give a damn what you want and neither will the new commandant.

**VLACO.** He'll only care about one thing:

**VLACO AND MALE CHORUS.** answers!

**AMINA.** Answers to what? They came to our village. They pulled us out of our house. They tore my dress. What answers can we give?

**VLACO.** Don't play stupid, Amina Jusic.

**VLACO AND MALE CHORUS.** Answers

**VLACO.** about the explosion at the fuel depot.

**VLACO AND THE MALE CHORUS.** Answers

**VLACO.** about hundreds of thousands of gallons of diesel gone.

**VLACO AND MALE CHORUS.** Answers

**VLACO.** About

**VLACO AND MALE CHORUS.** sabotage!

**AMINA.** We're village people. We know nothing.

**VLACO.** And you'd tell me if you did know something wouldn't you? You'd cooperate in a second, open right up like a dead clam. You'd tell me everything I asked.

**AMINA.** We heard the explosion like a thunder too close. Then the sky went black as if the

**AMINA AND THE FEMALE CHORUS.** eyes of God closed forever.

**AMINA.** We don't know anymore.

**SAMIRA.** We don't know how it happened. Leave her alone.

**VLACO AND THE MALE CHORUS.** Someone knows!

**VLACO.** A woman was seen walking away, from the depot shortly before the explosion. What kind of women live around here? What kind of women would have no qualms about burning

**VLACO AND MALE CHORUS.** Christian flesh?

**VLACO.** One of you.

**VLACO AND MALE CHORUS.** A Muslim woman.

**SAMIRA.** What Christian flesh?

(*VLACO takes her hand, places it on his.*)

**VLACO AND THE MALE CHORUS.** This Christian flesh.

(*SAMIRA pulls her hand away, pause.*)

**VLACO.** (*looking at the documents*) You're mother and daughter Amina and Samira Jusic.

**AMINA.** That's so.

**VLACO.** Where's your husband?

**AMINA.** Away.

**VLACO.** He's fighting.

**AMINA.** He's in the army. They left. The men all left. You know we don't know where.

**VLACO.** And your son as well? Also in the army?

**SAMIRA.** You invaded. Everyone became the army.

**AMINA.** Samira.

**SAMIRA.** Someone had to

**SAMIRA AND FEMALE CHORUS.** shoot back.

(*VLACO raises his hand to strike SAMIRA. AMINA comes between them.*)

**AMINA AND FEMALE CHORUS.** No!

**AMINA.** Don't. Don't. It's still raw in her mind. The ones from our village killed each year. She meant no disrespect. She's just angry.

**VLACO AND MALE CHORUS.** So am I angry!

**VLACO.** 16 soldiers roasted in that depot fire!

**VLACO AND MALE CHORUS.** Charcoal men! Unidentifiable!

**VLACO.** Black sooty charcoal men kissed goodnight by a car load of dynamite! But that means nothing to people like you, does it? They were just

**VLACO AND MALE CHORUS.** Serbs.

**VLACO.** Weren't they? Yes.

*(VLACO crosses back to the male chorus.)*

**JELA.** I told you about them here. They need little cause to lash out.

**AMINA.** Are you all right, daughter. You're shaking,

**JELA.** He would've punched you, you know.

**AMINA.** You can't talk back to them. Keep quiet and we'll come out of this, Samira. I know it.

**SAMIRA.** 16 soldiers were in the depot?

**JELA AND FEMALE CHORUS.** 16 less barbarians in the world

**JELA.** Who'll miss them

*(Lights fade. Sound punctuates.)*

**VLACO** *(addressing, the audience)* So many times, I begged

**VLACO AND MALE CHORUS.** God

**VLACO.** to

**VLACO AND MALE CHORUS.** forgive me for hating them.

**VLACO.** I knew how easily a man could turn cruel. I saw it in me.

**VLACO AND MALE CHORUS.** Dear Jesus,

**VLACO.** I prayed to him.

**VLACO AND MALE CHORUS.** Jesus, you understand

**VLACO.** I said. This is war and these are the fanatics who deny you,

**VLACO AND MALE CHORUS.** O Lord. Make me strong enough to control my anger at those who deny you.

*(Lights cross fade to AMINA and SAMIRA in their cell.)*

**AMINA.** This endless waiting, waiting, waiting, what can we tell them?…Samira, what's the matter?

**SAMIRA.** I didn't sleep at all last night. I can't sleep in this cage.

**AMINA.** Don't worry. Don't be afraid.

**SAMIRA.** I'm not afraid. I spent the whole night thinking of the soldiers in the depot. 16 boys burnt to nothing,

**AMINA AND FEMALE CHORUS.** God help us all

**AMINA.** I prayed myself asleep.

**SAMIRA AND FEMALE CHORUS.** Why were soldiers in the depot at that hour.

**AMINA.** Who knows. War doesn't have a time clock. It was their depot. Why're you surprised that troops were about?

**SAMIRA.** I thought at that time it would be locked up, closed down...that it would be...

**AMINA.** What? What is it?

(*JELA enters.*)

**JELA.** Sleep at all? It takes a while. Concrete for a mattress, I mean. (*She passes bread to them.*)

**AMINA.** Oh, thank you.

(**AMINA** *eats.* **SAMIRA** *does not.*)

What're you doing in this place?

**JELA.** They told me I was a potential danger to their military operation. That's what they told me when I asked.

**AMINA.** Why did they think that?

**JELA.** When they came through my village, they saw a slogan painted on a wall.

**JELA AND FEMALE CHORUS.** Serbs are shit. Watch were you walk.

**JELA.** They had no one to blame so they took me and my grandfather, because the wall was on our street and my grandfather smiled at their anger, when they saw the slogan. I don't know, where he is. Separated.

**JELA AND FEMALE CHORUS.** Separated.

**JELA.** Everyone in the country is

**JELA AND FEMALE CHORUS.** separated.

**JELA.** Everything in the world is

**JELA AND FEMALE CHORUS.** separated.

**AMINA.** And they don't say when you'll get out?

**JELA.** No. I've been punched, mauled, raped. And now

**JELA AND FEMALE CHORUS.** I'm a slave

**JELA.** in this camp.

**SAMIRA.** I don't want to stay here like that.

**SAMIRA AND FEMALE CHORUS.** I want to get out.

**SAMIRA.** Where are they?

**JELA.** Vlaco and the rest of them are getting ready for the new commandant. That's why they're not sniffing around. You know these army types always kissing the ass of someone higher up.

**AMINA.** Samira, eat...

**SAMIRA.** I can't, my stomach wants nothing

**JELA.** *(JELA looks around.)* Come close. Samira,

**JELA AND FEMALE CHORUS.** come close.

**JELA.** It's all right to talk to me. I know.

**AMINA.** You know what?

**JELA.** There are two of us in here who get messages in and out. My friend, Nadia, passed the information on to me. I know. I know. It's safe to talk to me.

*(She kisses SAMIRA's fingers.)*

**JELA AND FEMALE CHORUS.** God bless you

**JELA.** for what you did.

**JELA AND FEMALE CHORUS.** God bless you.

**AMINA.** What're you talking about? Samira...

*(SAMIRA backs away and turns her back.)*

Samira, what's she saying?

**JELA.** Keep your voice down. *(to SAMIRA)* Your mother doesn't know.

*(SAMIRA turns and nods her head "no.")*

Why? Why doesn't she...

**SAMIRA.** Don't you see? I'm a child to her, Jela.

**AMINA.** Are you saying...

**JELA.** Yes. Nadia got the word. It was your daughter who parked the car that blew the depot.

**AMINA.** Daughter...

**SAMIRA** *(turning)* Daughter, what? They killed my father and brother and they...

**AMINA.** You don't know that!

**AMINA AND FEMALE CHORUS.** Don't say that!

**SAMIRA.** After the battle outside Goradze, when we didn't hear from them again, what else could be the reason we hadn't heard from them again. So when these people approached me, I...I joined their group.

**AMINA.** What group?

**SAMIRA.** This group of women fighting the Serbs anyway we can.

**JELA.** I'm proud of you. Samira. Amina, they have no fuel now for their tanks and trucks in this area. Tanks and trucks full of troops that would've killed more Muslims. They're all proud of you. Samira.

**AMINA.** But you risked your life...

**JELA.** Might as well risk. I did nothing, but I'm here. I didn't even write that slogan on the wall. Be proud of your daughter.

**JELA AND FEMALE CHORUS.** She's a hero, Amina.

*(VLACO steps into the light and crosses to them.)*

**VLACO.** Go on. Go on with your bread.

**VLACO AND MALE CHORUS.** Stop plotting

**VLACO.** you'll not escape.

*(JELA crosses off.)*

**AMINA.** We weren't plotting. I want to see the commandant. Did you tell him I want to see him?

**VLACO.** The new commandant rests. He won't see anybody. But I will. *(sound of a cell door opening)* I need to question you both. *(to SAMIRA)* You first.

**AMINA.** My daughter's not well. She can't eat or sleep.

**AMINA AND FEMALE CHORUS.** Leave her alone.

**AMINA.** You can talk to me. Whatever she knows, I know. Lieutenant Vlaco,

**AMINA AND FEMALE CHORUS.** she's ill.

*(Long pause. AMINA leaves the cell. As AMINA and VLACO cross off, SAMIRA reaches out to her mother.)*

**SAMIRA.** God is great, mother.

**SAMIRA AND FEMALE CHORUS.** God be with you.

*(Lights fade on* **SAMIRA** *and* **AMINA**.*)*

**VLACO.** *(addressing the audience)* Some of the guards here do rape these women. I know it's wrong. I know. But its even encouraged here. Enemy women. It seems such a contradiction. A woman is a sister, a wife, a mother. A man's first drink of life is at a woman's breast.

*(A light comes up center as a soldier places a chair.* **AMINA** *sits.)*

But enemy women, madonnas who want to cut your throat. What's a man to make of this contradiction? He uses these women, lying in their soft, moist pouches merely to relieve himself. A perversion of women, of love, of life. (**VLACO** *crosses to* **AMINA**.*)*

…on Thursday evening, early, say between 6 and 6:30, what were you doing?

**AMINA.** I was home. Cooking. Rice and a few chicken thighs.

**VLACO.** On Thursday or the day before did you hear any one speak about the fuel depot in anyway, even in a joking way?

**VLACO AND MALE CHORUS.** I want to know everything, woman.

**AMINA.** I never heard a word. All we women talk about is our families and water and food and if the electric will come back. We did nothing

**VLACO.** When the blast went off, where were you?

**AMINA.** We were eating, daughter and me. We were eating. The floor shook, the windows rattled. Smoke, foul smelling smoke seeped into the house, we were scared.

**VLACO.** You were scared?

**AMINA.** Yes. Scared, that is was a shelling

**VLACO.** 16 men.

**VLACO AND MALE CHORUS.** 16 men

**VLACO.** were part of that foul smell.

**VLACO AND MALE CHORUS.** 16 men

**VLACO.** rode on that smoke that crept inside your houses to haunt this whole village until

**VLACO AND MALE CHORUS.** Justice

**VLACO.** is done!

**AMINA.** The whole war...the whole war's an atrocity. What can I say. You think I gloat over

**AMINA AND FEMALE CHORUS.** 16 men burnt alive?

**AMINA.** Well, I don't. Believe me, I don't.

**AMINA.** I have

**AMINA AND FEMALE CHORUS.** family

**AMINA.** in this war.

**VLACO.** About your daughter.

**AMINA.** She's a child.

**VLACO.** She doesn't look like a child to me.

**AMINA.** She is. She's not even 20 years old yet. She...She was with me. We were eating.

**VLACO.** What time was that?

**AMINA.** ...7:30. I know. I know because we always eat at 7:30. My husband always insisted we eat at 7:30, and we keep that schedule even though he and my son...

**VLACO.** Are where?

**AMINA.** I'm hoping to hear from them. I want to go home. I want to take my daughter out of this place. She's getting sick. *(pause)*

**FEMALE CHORUS.** I want to

**AMINA AND FEMALE CHORUS.** speak to the new commandant. I want to tell him my daughter's not well.

**VLACO.** Colonel Herak is not well himself. He's not seeing anyone.

**AMINA.** Colonel Herak?

**FEMALE CHORUS.** *(whisper)* Branislav Herak.

**AMINA.** *(pause)* Branislav Herak – who taught at the University before the war.

**AMINA AND FEMALE CHORUS.** Branislav Herak...

**VLACO.** Forget Colonel Herak. I want to know about your daughter.

AMINA. Why harp on her? What could she know?

VLACO. On Thursday what time did she come home?

AMINA. I don't know exactly.

VLACO. Where was she?

AMINA. She was with friends, young friends. They sit and giggle and act silly. Some of them are in here on the other side of the camp She was home with me at 7:30.

VLACO. But the explosives were on a timing, device. It could've been set a half hour or an hour ahead.

AMINA. Samira's a teen-aged girl. What does she know about timing devices?

VLACO. It's a simple matter to teach a person to set a timing device, Amina Jusic. Even a child could do it.

VLACO AND MALE CHORUS. Even a young, teen-aged girl.

AMINA. She was

AMINA AND FEMALE CHORUS. home. Home

AMINA. with me. How many times do you want me to say it?

AMINA. Why would she do such a thing? Why would she cause such destruction?

VLACO. Why? Why, Amina Jusic, wife of Ekrem Jusic and Mother of Vedran Jusic?

VLACO AND MALE CHORUS. For the cause.

AMINA. What cause?

VLACO. It's a war.

VLACO AND MALE CHORUS. The cause of war.

AMINA AND FEMALE CHORUS. We have no cause.

AMINA. We just want to go back to living in peace the way we did before you came here.

AMINA AND FEMALE CHORUS. She has no cause.

VLACO. Then how long had she been home on Thursday? You said she was with her friends.

AMINA. She…she was…she was and then…and then she…

AMINA AND FEMALE CHORUS. she came home.

VLACO AND MALE CHORUS. What time?

AMINA. I don't know.

**FEMALE CHORUS.** The power was out.

**AMINA.** The clock stopped. But it was long before we ate at 7:30.

**VLACO.** How'd you know it was 7:30?

**AMINA.** By...

**FEMALE CHORUS.** by the light...

**AMINA.** by the dying light of day that fell in the kitchen.

**AMINA AND FEMALE CHORUS.** She was home.

**VLACO.** Why wasn't she home earlier to help you cook?

**AMINA.** She...she can't cook.

**VLACO AND MALE CHORUS.** A good Muslim girl of 19 can't cook?

**AMINA.** I mean she's not a good cook. She came home and...and she went to lie down. I'd...I'd rather cook myself.

**VLACO.** Amina Jusic, before the war I was a policeman. I've questioned many people. I've sat across the table from countless liars. People who tell the truth bore me. I send them home. Yes, home. My interest is in finding

**VLACO AND MALE CHORUS.** liars,

**VLACO.** Amina Jusic.

**VLACO AND MALE CHORUS.** Liars. Liars

**VLACO.** hold a hidden truth. All I have to do is open that little locket of equivocation and I have a picture of the truth.

**AMINA.** I'm not

**VLACO AND MALE CHORUS.** Lying! Lying! Goddamned lying!

**VLACO.** Lying's an internal struggle for a human being. Most people who aren't psychopaths are not used to lying big. About

**VLACO AND MALE CHORUS.** life and death,

**VLACO.** I mean. So when people lie big, there's a jet of stress that shoots through them. Their voices. Their hands. Their eyes – do you know even eye blinks, Amina Jusic, give away this little skirmish in one's heart?

**AMINA.** Think what you like. You're wrong. I know nothing and

**AMINA AND FEMALE CHORUS.** I have no cause. *(pause)*

**VLACO.** Amina Jusic,

**VLACO AND MALE CHORUS.** take off your dress.

**AMINA.** What?

**VLACO.** Your dress!

**VLACO AND MALE CHORUS.** Remove your dress!

**AMINA.** will not.

**VLACO.** Some of the guards here would walk into this room and, without a word, punch hard your face on the cheek bone. Your face numbs up and stuns you. The rape after that is much easier, Amina Jusic.

**AMINA.** Don't...don't do this.

**VLACO.** Remove your dress, must I tear it off you?

**AMINA AND FEMALE CHORUS.** How could you call yourself a Christian and do this? How?

**VLACO.** What does that have to do with it? What does

**VLACO AND MALE CHORUS.** Christ mean to someone like you?

**VLACO.** How dare you who don't worship him use him to defend your O so sacred skin?

**VLACO AND MALE CHORUS.** Remove your dress!

**AMINA.** I'll report this to the commandant. Colonel Herak's not a man who'd allow this.

**VLACO.** You think Colonel Herak gives a damn about you?

**AMINA.** I can't believe such a man wouldn't care.

**VLACO.** Don't you know what Muslim men do to our women when they get their hands on them. I've seen the results, Amina Jusic.

**AMINA AND FEMALE CHORUS.** It's wrong! It's wrong!

**AMINA.** Whoever does this! All of it is wrong!

**AMINA AND FEMALE CHORUS.** Stop it!

**VLACO.** No one can stop it.

**VLACO AND MALE CHORUS.** How many has your husband raped?

**VLACO.** or even your son?

**AMINA AND FEMALE CHORUS.** None! None!

**AMINA.** They would never do this!

**VLACO AND MALE CHORUS.** Remove your dress!

**VLACO.** I could rip it from your body, but I want you to remove it.

**AMINA AND FEMALE CHORUS.** No.

**AMINA.** In the name of the

**AMINA AND FEMALE CHORUS.** compassionate merciful God,

**AMINA.** please, don't.

**AMINA AND FEMALE CHORUS.** Please.

**AMINA.** I can't do such a thing.

**VLACO.** You can't. You can't. So you can't. Well, maybe your

**VLACO AND MALE CHORUS.** teen-aged daughter

**VLACO.** will be more

**VLACO AND MALE CHORUS.** forthcoming.

**AMINA.** Lieutenant, she's my child.

**VLACO.** She's a child with

**VLACO AND MALE CHORUS.** hips and breasts,

**VLACO.** a ripe child. Listen to me. I knew some of the men in that depot. Some were combat engineers making repairs on the pipes. Some were guards. Young boys, and they could act silly too and talk about home and think about girls. Now they're dead. So don't tell me how loving and caring your people are.

**VLACO AND MALE CHORUS.** Your child. Your child.

**VLACO.** I'll just go and

**VLACO AND MALE CHORUS.** fetch your child.

**AMINA AND FEMALE CHORUS.** No!

**AMINA.** She's not well. She's…she's sick…

**AMINA AND FEMALE CHORUS.** let me speak – to the Colonel…please.

**VLACO AND MALE CHORUS.** I ask you one last time…

**AMINA AND FEMALE CHORUS.** I want to see the colonel.

**VLACO AND MALE CHORUS.** Remove your dress or I'll remove hers!

*(Pause. **VLACO** begins to exit. **AMINA** stops him again. Slowly she removes her dress. She stands in her slip.)*

**VLACO.** You see. You see how, easy it is? Do you know why you did it? Do you? You did it because

**VLACO AND MALE CHORUS.** you had a cause.

**VLACO.** Yes, You see how easy it is to sacrifice anything when

**VLACO AND MALE CHORUS.** you have a cause.

**VLACO.** I want to *(He grabs her and pulls her close.)*

**VLACO AND MALE CHORUS.** punch you and rape you, Amina Jusic. *(Suddenly, he pulls away and speaks to himself.)*

**VLACO.** But it is a sin and I am a

**VLACO AND MALE CHORUS.** Christian.

**VLACO.** Unlike some of the others here.

**VLACO AND MALE CHORUS.** my faith in Christ won't let me.

**VLACO.** Do you understand? Get down on your knees and thank

**VLACO AND MALE CHORUS.** Jesus Christ.

**VLACO.** You won't be raped today because of Him. Get down! *(She kneels.)*

**VLACO AND MALE CHORUS.** Thank him! Thank Jesus! Thank him!

**AMINA AND FEMALE CHORUS.** Thank you, Jesus. Thank you, Jesus.

**AMINA.** Thank you!

*(Lights fade. Music punctuates.)*

**VLACO.** *(**VLACO** slowly walks towards the audience and addresses them.)* I served with some of those in the fuel depot. And anger is a human trait. That I'm not perfect proves that I need almighty God, the perfection of us all.

*(A light comes up on **COLONEL BRANISLAV HERAK**. A soldier brings him a wheel chair. He sits. **VLACO** crosses him.)*

Colonel Branislav Herak, soon to be General, and who knows, perhaps, even president of Serbia some day. Right now he is recovering from battle wounds.

*(VLACO begins pushing the wheel chair. HERAK quick-ens. Lights come up on AMINA and SAMIRA in their cell. VLACO wheels the chair by and stops.)*

**VLACO.** ...and in 37 is a mother and daughter,

**VLACO.** picked up after the depot attack.

**AMINA.** Colonel,...you're...you're Colonel Herak...

**AMINA AND FEMALE CHORUS.** Branislav Herak...

**HERAK.** I am...you look so familiar.

**AMINA.** I'm Amina. That's why I'm familiar to you. I'm Amina Sacirhev. My married name's now, Jusic.

**HERAK.** Amina Sacirhev. Good God, yes. Yes, your father was Mohammed Sacirhev,

**AMINA.** Who had the farm.

**HERAK.** I took training here, Lieutenant. When I was young, a group of us use to go down to her father's farm to buy eggs and cheese. Yes. Amina Sacirhev.

**AMINA.** What happened to you? Is it your legs?

**HERAK.** No. I can walk. I'm recuperating from an operation.

**AMINA.** Samira,

**AMINA AND FEMALE CHORUS.** he remembers me.

**AMINA.** This is my daughter, Samira, Colonel. They arrested us both.

**HERAK.** The destruction of the fuel depot. It's a grave matter. You understand. Everyone has to be questioned.

**AMINA.** They did question me. But we're still being held.

**VLACO.** We're not finished with them. Sir. The daughter's been ill. We haven't talked to her yet and...

**HERAK.** And what?

**VLACO AND MALE CHORUS.** I think this woman knows something.

**AMINA.** We know nothing. Colonel, you must believe me.

**AMINA AND FEMALE CHORUS.** You must help us.

**AMINA.** Please, we want to go home.

**AMINA AND FEMALE CHORUS.** Help us.

**HERAK** *(to* **VLACO***)* Bring her to my quarters at noon.

*(as* **VLACO** *wheels the chair off)*

**VLACO.** Yes, Sir.

**AMINA.** Thank you. Thank you, Colonel. Samira, he'll help us.

**SAMIRA.** He's a Serb Colonel. Herak. Herak. He's one of the worse butchers in the Serb army.

**AMINA.** I knew him when he was a boy. He and his friends couldn't stomach army food. Your grandfather sold them milk and cheese and eggs. So many years ago and he remembers. Oh, Samira.

**AMINA AND FEMALE CHORUS.** he remembers. God

**AMINA.** is great.

**AMINA AND FEMALE CHORUS.** God

**AMINA.** watches over us.

**AMINA AND FEMALE CHORUS.** God is answering my Prayers. Branislav Herak will help us.

**SAMIRA.** He's the enemy, mother. He's Vlaco with more brass on his uniform. I don't care how much milk he bought from grandfather. He's a Serb.

**AMINA.** But

**AMINA AND FEMALE CHORUS.** he remembers…

**AMINA.** don't you understand?

*(Lights fade. Sound punctuates. Music.)*

**VLACO.** *(addressing the audience)* Milk. He bought milk here years and years ago. For centuries cattle grazed the land where we now have this camp. Perhaps some of the cattle that fed here made the milk that rests in the bones of Branislav Herak. There was a small cabin on the spot. When we took this area and fenced in the camp, the cabin became the commandant's billet. It's more comfortable than any place in the camp.

*(Lights come up on* **HERAK** *behind a table in his wheel chair and* **AMINA** *sitting in a chair.)*

That day at noon I personally brought Amina Jusic to the Colonel.

**AMINA.** *(as they quicken)* ...and even before the fire was put out they dragged us from our houses. All the women in the area. Pulling us by our hair. Kicking us. Butting us without mercy, with their rifles. My daughter and I know nothing. When can we go home?

**HERAK.** Until we find the women responsible for this, nobody can go anywhere.

**AMINA.** You're God here. You can do anything

**HERAK.** Of course. I can. I could send you through the gate right now. But I won't. Of all the women taken, some one here must know something. Some one will talk soon, and the innocent will be released. Are you being mistreated here?

**AMINA AND FEMALE CHORUS.** *(as AMINA rises)* Mistreated.

**AMINA.** We get stale bread. No chance to wash up.

**AMINA.** And I was

**AMINA AND FEMALE CHORUS.** forced

**AMINA.** to take my clothes off.

**HERAK.** Who did that?

**HERAK.** I want to know. Which of the guards did this?

**AMINA.** I don't want to say. I didn't even tell my daughter. I just want you to know. This is not just a place to wait for questioning.

**AMINA AND FEMALE CHORUS.** It's a prison.

**HERAK.** I won't tolerate my soldiers doing this. Just give me his name.

**AMINA.** I won't. I won't because I fear for my daughter. She's too young to be in a place like this. It's making her sick.

**AMINA AND FEMALE CHORUS.** I'm afraid.

**AMINA.** I'm afraid. Colonel. What am I going to do?

**HERAK.** Where's your family? Your husband?

**AMINA** *(taking out her picture)* This is my husband, Ekrem, and my son, Vedran. Jusic is the family name. I don't know where they are. If they're being held some-place...if you could find them for me...

**AMINA.** Find out where they are, at least.

**HERAK.** I'll make some inquiries. I can't guarantee anything

**AMINA.** But you'll

**AMINA AND FEMALE CHORUS.** try to find them.

**HERAK.** As soon as I feel a little better.

**AMINA.** What happened to you?

**HERAK.** Shrapnel. You never think you can be hit. You stand and direct your men and fear for them but never for yourself. Oh. it's not bravery, no. It's arrogance. You just don't ever imagine yourself dying. Life is too rich for one to die. There's yet too much to do to even consider But then, when the flying metal opened my stomach, I knew, it was one of death's claws tearing, at my insides.

**HERAK AND MALE CHORUS.** Death is real now.

**HERAK.** He swiped his paws it me. I'm only here in this camp to recuperate. And then back to…to the fight.

**AMINA.** Why? God,

**AMINA AND FEMALE CHORUS.** why this Fight? Why this Fight?

**HERAK.** Why this fight. We've been asking that for thousands of years. Politics. It's always politics. War is politics gone mad. Guns to do what words couldn't. You know what happened in World War II. Your people and the Croats, they teamed with the Nazis. They tried to exterminate us. Serbs and Jews. Us and the Jews.

**HERAK AND MALE CHORUS.** They made no distinction,

**HERAK.** Amina,

**HERAK AND MALE CHORUS.** between Serbs and Jews.

**HERAK.** After that war the peace was…was artificial. But when the country broke up, we couldn't sit still and wait for the massacre to begin again. Why, you ask? Why this fight? Whose version do you want? To you, we're

**HERAK AND FEMALE CHORUS.** invaders.

**HERAK.** To us we're

**HERAK AND MALE CHORUS.** defenders.

**AMINA.** So the World War never ended.

**HERAK.** Not here.

**HERAK AND MALE CHORUS.** And it won't end until all...

**AMINA.** Go on and say it. It won't end until all the

**AMINA AND FEMALE CHORUS.** Muslims are dead..

**AMINA.** Say it That's why, I'm afraid for my family. This camp is a field of snakes. There's hate in every glance and stare.

**FEMALE CHORUS.** Branislav *(whisper)*

**AMINA.** I want to call you Branislav now.

**HERAK.** You may go Lieutenant. *(VLACO exits.)*

**AMINA.** Please, do me one favor.

**HERAK.** If I can.

**AMINA.** If we're going to be held here for a while, please... please,

**AMINA AND FEMALE CHORUS.** take my daughter

**AMINA.** on in here with you as a housekeeper during the day.

**HERAK.** A housekeeper? Why would you want her to...

**AMINA.** Because, she'll be safe working in here. You have women outside sweeping. I saw the little kitchen in there. She can cook and clean up. She's a good cook, and she'll be away from...I mean...

**AMINA AND FEMALE CHORUS.** no one would touch your housekeeper...Please.

**HERAK.** I don't think it's such a good idea, Amina.

**AMINA.** Why not?

*(VLACO enters with a tray of food and puts it down.)*

**HERAK.** You see. I have people to look after me. I have a corporal who cooks and a lieutenant who wants to be a captain. Thank you. Lieutenant. And you can have the sergeant at the door escort Amina Jusic back now. *(to AMINA)*

**HERAK AND MALE CHORUS.** Don't be afraid.

**HERAK.** No harm will come to you or your daughter.

*(AMINA looks at VLACO.)*

**AMINA.** Thank you. Think you for seeing me. I do feel better now.

*(VLACO escorts AMINA off. HERAK rises with a cup of coffee from the tray. VLACO re-enters.)*

**HERAK.** Lieutenant.

**VLACO.** Yes, Sir.

**HERAK.** Can't you find some fruit for these women?

**VLACO.** We're trying. Sir. Since the depot explosion, we're over loaded with prisoners.

**HERAK** *(picking up an apple from the tray)* Where did this come from?

**VLACO.** Our mess.

**HERAK.** Well, give these women some. And showers. Let them use the showers.

**VLACO.** We're getting around to arranging a schedule. We don't have much in the way of facilities.

**HERAK.** So I noticed this morning. By the way, Lieutenant, who interrogated this Jusic woman?

**VLACO.** I did, Sir.

**HERAK.** Oh, and what did you find out?

**VLACO.** She won't say anything, but I have a notion that she's holding back. I can tell. Either she knows something or she knows her daughter knows something.

**HERAK.** I see. Then we'll eventually have to get around to the daughter, I suppose.

**VLACO.** Definitely, Colonel. Definitely.

*(Lights fade. Sound punctuates.)*

**VLACO.** *(addressing the audience)* The daughter. Samira. The daughter's skin was light brown and always looked moist, as If it had just been rubbed with oil. Her eyes were big almond eyes, and her face gave an instant flush to men's desire. A priest would say the

**VLACO AND MALE CHORUS.** devil had spoken to these men

**VLACO.** to jar their lusts. Several of the guards had already heeded the devil and planned

**VLACO AND MALE CHORUS.** to take Samira Jusic.

*(Lights come up on* **AMINA** *and* **SAMIRA** *standing in their cell.* **JELA** *etnters with the bread bag and on her shoulder and a small sack of apples.* **AMINA** *and* **SAMIRA** *quicken.* **JELA** *hands them bread and an apple each.)*

**JELA.** It's out.

**AMINA.** What's out?

**JELA.** It's out that you know Herak.

**AMINA.** When he was a boy years ago.

**SAMIRA.** A lot of good it does us

**JELA.** He was civil to her. He ordered the fruit, and you're going to get to use the shower.

**AMINA.** How'd you find that out?

**JELA.** The women sweeping outside his cabin. They heard him tell Vlaco.

**SAMIRA.** So what, Jela? So we got an apple. We're still in this

**SAMIRA AND FEMALE CHORUS.** damned cage.

**JELA.** It seems like nothing to you. But it could be to our advantage that he'll listen to her. It could be that...

*(***VLACO** *enters the scene.* **JELA** *looks at him. Then she scurries off. He crosses to the cell and opens it.)*

**AMINA.** What is it now?

**VLACO.** You asked for showers, didn't you? The Colonel said you should have showers...now...

*(***AMINA** *and* **SAMIRA** *start to exit the cell.* **VLACO** *stops* **SAMIRA.***)*

One at a time. There's only one shower pipe, you're not going to cuddle under it.

*(***AMINA** *hesitates.)*

You bitched for showers.

**SAMIRA.** It's not a special favor to be decent.

**AMINA.** Samira, be quiet.

**SAMIRA.** Go ahead, mother. You go first. You won't be that long.

VLACO. Better take your scarf with you. We have no towels.

(AMINA *takes her scarf and exits.*)

It always amuses me how you women seek for decency in a war.

VLACO AND MALE CHORUS. War is decency's enemy,

VLACO. and blows up with the first shell fired.

SAMIRA. And who started the war? Who fired the first shell into the mouth of decency?

VLACO. Muslims always play the innocents. When the country broke up, how many Arab states pissed money to you to attack us?

SAMIRA. Not until you threatened. Someone has to

SAMIR AND FEMALE CHORUS. help us.

VLACO. Not someone.

VLACO AND MALE CHORUS. Your own kind.

VLACO. The Islamics.

VLACO AND MALE CHORUS. Your brother in Allah.

VLACO. No one else matters.

SAMIRA. And no

SAMIRA AND FEMALE CHORUS. Christian money

SAMIRA. paid for the pistol on your belt?

VLACO. And what money paid for the Citroen loaded with explosives that sent up our fuel depot?

(SARMIRA *turns away.*)

Who organized it? Who? Who? What do you know? Who, you little

VLACO AND MALE CHORUS. bitch. Tell me what you know!
(*He turns her around.*)

SAMIRA. What? What can I tell, you?

VLACO. The names of those responsible. The name of the woman who drove that car.

SAMIRA. I never heard a word. I was at home.

VLACO. What time? Thursday.

VLACO AND MALE CHORUS. Think.

**SAMIRA.** Early. I was home early. I cooked some…what was it…some chicken bones and rice for supper.

**VLACO.** You cooked?

**SAMIRA.** Some chicken and rice, yes.

**VLACO.** Are you a good cook?

**SAMIRA.** Yes, my grandmother taught me.

**VLACO AND MALE CHORUS.** You and your mother know something.

**SAMIRA.** Know what?

**VLACO AND MALE CHORUS.** About 16 dead soldiers.

**SAMIRA.** It's a shame. It's such a shame. I feel so sorry for them. I do. But I don't know,…don't know who…

**VLACO.** You're lying.

**VLACO AND MALE CHORUS.** Muslims lie the way some people breath,

**VLACO.** as a matter of life. (**VLACO** *takes hold of the hem of her dress.*)

**SAMIRA AND FEMALE CHORUS.** Keep away from me!

**VLACO.** They'll come for you. The guards love the look of you. They take great delight in riding the arrogance out of a young bitch. They'll open that

**VLACO AND MALE CHORUS.** little virgin patch like a ripe peach…

**SAMIRA AND FEMALE CHORUS.**

(*as* **HERAK** *wheels in on his chair*)

Let go of my dress!

**SAMIRA.** I'll pull one of your eyes out!

**SAMIRA AND FEMALE CHORUS.** Let go!

**VLACO AND MALE CHORUS.** Tell me what you know

**VLACO.** and I'll protect you from them.

**SAMIRA AND FEMALE CHORUS.** Stop this!

**HERAK.** Lieutenant!

(**VLACO** *releases her and turns to* **HERAK.**)

**VLACO AND MALE CHORUS.** Sir. I think these two are hiding information.

(**AMINA** *returns drying her hair with her scarf.*)

**HERAK.** And you were just gathering that information from her with your hand up her dress.

**VLACO.** I was trying to get her to talk, Sir.

**AMINA.** What is it? What's the matter? Samira?

**SAMIRA.** I'm not hurt, mother. I'm not hurt.

**AMINA** (*looking, at* **VLACO**) Because the Colonel came by.

**HERAK.** Go about your duties, Lieutenant. I'll lock this cell up. And when you're finished, I'd like to see you.

**VLACO.** Yes, Sir. (**VLACO** *exits.*)

**AMINA.** Thank you, Colonel.

**SAMIRA.** Thank you, Colonel? Why thank him? It's only a matter of time before they rape all of us.

**SAMIRA AND FEMALE CHORUS.** All of us.

**SAMIRA.** You expect him to come by every time one of these animals wants

**SAMIRA AND FEMALE CHORUS.** to fight the war with his dick?! Stop thanking him!

**AMINA.** Colonel, you see how it is?

**HERAK.** Go take your shower now.

(**AMINA** *hands* **SAMIRA** *the scarf.* **SAMIRA** *shakes her head and exits.*)

**HERAK.** (*to* **AMINA**) I'll speak to the Lieutenant and…

**AMINA.** It won't matter who you speak to. My daughter's right. This time…this time you came by. I'm afraid now more than before

**AMINA AND FEMALE CHORUS.** I'm afraid.

**HERAK.** Lieutenant Vlaco's convinced that you and your daughter know something about the depot explosion.

**AMINA.** Us? Nothing. No. We…we just get so scared when he asks all those questions that we stumble and he thinks we're holding back. It's just fright. That's why I beg you to take Samira on as a housekeeper. If you won't let us go home, do me this kindness.

**AMINA AND FEMALE CHORUS.** Please.

**HERAK.** I don't want anyone as a housekeeper.

**AMINA.** You see how pretty she is. If you don't help, one of them will get to her. I see the way they look at her.

**AMINA AND FEMALE CHORUS.** They'll get her one day alone.

**HERAK.** I've given the order that no woman in this camp who's obeying the regulations is to be mistreated.

**AMINA.** A man who's out to rape doesn't care about orders. And what woman is going to report the man or men, what would happen to her after that?

**HERAK.** This…this is not an easy command for me. I'm a field officer. But I promise I'll do my best to…

**AMINA.** Good intentions won't help. Some of those men are vicious…I can see to

**AMINA AND FEMALE CHORUS.** save my daughter,

**AMINA.** I must tell you.

**HERAK AND MALE CHORUS.** Tell me what?

*(AMINA kneels in front of his chair.)*

**AMINA.** I tell you about me only to

**AMINA AND FEMALE CHORUS.** save my daughter.

**AMINA.** She would die before she'd let one of your men take her like that…

**AMINA AND FEMALE CHORUS.** She would die,

**AMINA.** I tell you.

**HERAK.** I understand, but…

**AMINA.** You don't understand. Twenty…twenty years ago when you left this dot on the map of Yugoslavia you…

**HERAK.** What? What is it?

**AMINA.** You left me…

**AMINA AND FEMALE CHORUS.** Samira.

**HERAK.** *(backing up his chair)* What?

**AMINA.** Yes.

**HERAK.** I left you…what…what possessed you to make up a story, like this? I've heard of people doing anything when desperate, but if you expect me to…

**AMINA.** I tell you the

**AMINA AND FEMALE CHORUS.** truth.

**AMINA.** You believe what you will. But before you disbelieve, recall that summer afternoon when two young people in the thick grass of these fields gave love to one another. *(pause)* Did I make that up, Colonel?

**AMINA AND FEMALE CHORUS.** Did I?

**HERAK.** No. Of course, I remember. The day before my battalion left.

**AMINA.** Yes, your last day. You told me you'd never forget me and I knew you wouldn't, and I said the same, and I never forgot you. I cried so much when you left...

**HERAK.** Amina...

**AMINA.** How I cried...

**FEMALE CHORUS.** How beautiful, how sad.

**AMINA.** Later, when I found out that I carried your child, I panicked. My father would have...I was sure I'd be killed. A strict Muslim...I'm sure he would've found some way to kill me. It's been done in our village before, you know. Girls are killed for such things. And with you,

**AMINA AND FEMALE CHORUS.** a Serb.

**AMINA.** Even then father hated the...the...

**HERAK.** I understand.

**AMINA.** Ekrem, my husband, always loved me. When I went to him and told him, he married me right away. He saved me. I love him so much. I wish he were here with me...

**HERAK.** Daughter? This girl? This

**HERAK AND MALE CHORUS.** Samira Jusic?

**AMINA.** Branislav, how could I invent such a story? Such a lie? You remember the day.

**HERAK.** I said I did. But you still could've concocted this...

**AMINA.** *(moving closer to him)* Look at me. Do you think I made it up? Look.

**AMINA AND FEMALE CHORUS.** Look at me.

**AMINA.** Look past the wrinkled skin. See into my eyes. See back to the young people. Their first love. Their passion that like opium made a pleasure of their short time together. Remember.

**AMINA AND FEMALE CHORUS.** Remember.

**AMINA.** *(pause)* And now twenty years later, do you think I'd violate all that's holy between me and my husband by giving his daughter to you in a lie? *(long pause)* Branislav...

**HERAK.** I search your eyes, but I don't know, Amina. The eyes don't go back to the soul, only back to the optic nerve. You told a lie to your father twenty years ago...A monumental lie,

**HERAK AND MALE CHORUS.** a monumental lie to save your life.

**HERAK.** Would you tell another now to save your daughter's'

**AMINA.** Branislav, listen to...Samira.

> *(SAMIRA resumes drying her hair.* **AMINA** *rises* **SAMIRA** *re-enters the cell.* **HERAK** *regards them both. Then he locks the cell and wheels himself off. Lights fade. Sound punctuates. Music.)*

**VLACO.** *(addressing the audience)* To the great Herak, the sly, brilliant military strategist, this was a temporary assignment. To him it was not part of the war, just an unpleasant duty between campaigns until he recovered.

> *(***HERAK** *slowly rolls his wheel chair across the stage to his cabin. He pauses briefly as* **VLACO** *references him and the continues.)*

He'd never been in command of a detention camp like this. A camp for women no less. A camp where an old love and her daughter turned up. Amina's words struck him like another war wound...

> *(***VLACO** *crosses into the light.* **HERAK** *consumed with thought does not see him.)*

**VLACO.** Colonel...

**HERAK.** Oh, yes, come in.

**VLACO.** About this morning...

**HERAK.** About this morning. Yes. Yes, this girl...this Jusic girl...

**VLACO.** I think she knows something. My police dog nose twitches when I see her.

**HERAK.** More than your nose twitched this morning, Lieutenant.

**VLACO.** I was merely trying to pressure her, Sir. I was trying to scare her a bit.

**HERAK.** Be that as it may, we will extract information from these women by interrogation not by brutality. We'll be methodical but professional, persistent but not inhuman. Do I make myself clear?

**VLACO.** Yes, Sir. I always thought of our men here as human.

**HERAK.** Well, perhaps, some of these detained women think of us as inhuman when we remove their clothes... Think of us as

**HERAK AND ½ MALE CHORUS.** savages

**HERAK.** when we

**HERAK AND ½ MALE CHORUS.** rape them.

**VLACO.** I won't deny it goes on, Sir.

**HERAK.** I can see it in these women's faces. I can see it goes on here. And I know all sides – The Croats, the Muslims – and, yes, us, we all have these...these lapses in human decency, but...*(He holds his stomach as if a pain came to him.)*

**VLACO.** Are you all right, Sir?

**HERAK.** I'm all right. It's my wound reminding me of the war. The

**HERAK AND MALE CHORUS.** pain of war's

**HERAK.** inside me now. Lieutenant. *(He sits in his chair.)* I'll mend. I just wish it didn't take so damned long. Stuck here while my guts mend. In a women's camp...what was I saying?

**VLACO.** Lapses. Lapses is human decency.

**HERAK.** Yes. Yes. No more, Lieutenant. No more rape here.

**HERAK AND MALE CHORUS.** None.

**HERAK.** Do you hear me, Lieutenant?

**VLACO.** I understand, Sir. I understand you're not used to this.

**HERAK.** Used to what? What is it you want to say? Speak up, Lieutenant.

**VLACO.** I just...I just want to point out to the Colonel that I can give that order, but no one can over see what every guard does twenty four hours a day. There's rancor, Sir, in the hearts of these men.

**VLACO AND ½ MALE CHORUS.** Rancor and vengeance are human too.

**VLACO.** They saw what was done to their own kind.

**HERAK.** What own kind? These are

**HERAK AND ½ MALE CHORUS.** helpless women.

**HERAK.** Some of them are still

**HERAK AND ½ MALE CHORUS.** children.

**VLACO.** All I'm saying is that you can issue an order to

**VLACO AND ½ MALE CHORUS.** hold back the sea,

**VLACO.** Sir. but the sea might wash right over you...

**HERAK.** Lieutenant Vlaco..

**VLACO.** Sir?

**HERAK AND MALE CHORUS.** Hold back the sea

**HERAK.** or it will wash over you.

**VLACO.** I'll give the order, Sir, but...

**HERAK.** But what? *(pause)* Are you afraid to talk to me? What is it?

**VLACO.** Sir, some of these men served with you in the 9th regiment.

**HERAK.** As well as you. Lieutenant.

**VLACO.** Yes, Sir, as well as I. Some of them last night talked about Sonja's Kon-Tiki.

**HERAK.** The Kon-Tiki, the bar, yes. So?

**VLACO.** So...well...it...it was also a brothel, Sir. In the back. The front was a bar, but in the back...anyway, they talked about how you visited Sonja's...

**HERAK.** *(rising)* Lieutenant...

**VLACO.** Sir, I have to tell you what they're saying.

**HERAK.** I hadn't...I hadn't seen my wife in months. I paid... I paid, yes. Yes, I did...I paid.

**VLACO.** As many of the officers of the 9th did. But those women, Sir, were Croat and Muslim girls.

**HERAK AND ½ MALE CHORUS.** I paid those girls.

**VLACO.** They were forced to perform for us or...or

**VLACO AND ½ MALE CHORUS.** they were shot.

**VLACO.** The money went to Sonja's...I'm saying this to you, because the men last night were relieved that you were in command here. They said

**VLACO AND ½ MALE CHORUS.** Herak understands how it is.

**VLACO.** Sir, when I tell them to keep their hands off these women, they'll bring it up. Sonja's, I mean. The girls at Sonja's. I was there when one of them refused to go into the back where those smelly little rooms were, powder and cheap perfume. The next day when we went by in convoy – you remember – we saw her – the one who refused. Her body just off the road. I remember you stopped and looked and...

**HERAK.** *(as HERAK turns away)* She was

**HERAK AND MALE CHORUS.** no older than 14.

**HERAK.** I can still see her. Legs one way, arms another. An old sweater and skirt thrown with no reverence on the side of a dirt road...Her wide eyes looked shocked...

**HERAK AND ½ MALE CHORUS.** Her open mouth

**HERAK.** trying to shout something...trying to shout something from death. Trying to call us

**HERAK AND ½ MALE CHORUS.** beasts.

**HERAK.** Trying to curse us from the hear-after for what they -

**½ MALE CHORUS.** we –

**HERAK AND ½ MALE CHORUS.** did.

**HERAK AND FEMALE CHORUS.** Savage! Savage!

**HERAK AND MALE CHORUS.** She screamed at me.

**HERAK.** Savage bastards!

**FEMALE CHORUS.** Savage bastards! *(Repeat four times.)*

**HERAK.** Was I the only one who heard her?

**VLACO.** I didn't mean to upset you, Colonel. It's just that the men...the men have seen Serbian women lying in dirt just like that girl. I know it's terrible. I agree. But sometimes in war men...men lose their senses...It's human to lose your senses. You take that Jusic girl.

*(HERAK turns to him.)*

**VLACO AND MALE CHORUS.** The men look at her, a beautiful girl

**VLACO.** and yet the enemy.

**VLACO AND ½ MALE CHORUS.** A Muslim.

**VLACO.** They feel they can do anything they want to the enemy. They feel that they...

**HERAK.** You're not married, Lieutenant, or have a family yet.

**VLACO.** No, Sir.

**HERAK.** They might be the enemy, but I see something else in Amina Jusic and her daughter.

**HERAK AND ½ MALE CHORUS.** I see a frightened parent trying to protect her child.

**HERAK.** I'm not a police officer, Lieutenant, but I'm acute enough to pick up that this Amina and Samira Jusic are two scared rabbits. I interrogated them this morning and I conclude that they

**HERAK AND ½ MALE CHORUS.** don't know anything

**HERAK.** about the fuel depot explosion.

**VLACO.** But, Colonel, we must interrogate them under the pressure of...

**HERAK.** And furthermore...Further more, I've been thinking, Lieutenant that...That I need a housekeeper in here.

**VLACO.** A housekeeper?

**HERAK.** Your Corporal's coffee tastes like water through a gravel pit and he burned my eggs.

**VLACO.** I'm sorry for that, Sir, but...

**HERAK.** I'll have this – what's her name – Samira Jusic workin here during the day as a housekeeper.

**VLACO.** Her? You want her in here?

**HERAK.** Yes.

**VLACO.** In your private quarters?

**VLACO.** Free to move about the kitchen, the bedroom?

**HERAK.** If she's going to make up my bed and cook me a bite to eat, I would think so. I'm not about to nail her to the wall.

**VLACO.** Sir. you don't need me to point out to you that these women are Muslims. The enemy. Pretty face or fawning attitude, they are the other side, Sir. There are knives in the kitchen, and there's a pistol in your belt. and there's…

**HERAK.** I'm a soldier, Lieutenant, and she's…she's a young village girl. *(He sits again.)* I'm sure I can defend myself.

**VLACO.** Sir…

**HERAK.** I don't want to

**HERAK AND ½ MALE CHORUS.** discuss it further.

**HERAK AND ALL MALE CHORUS.** See that she's here in the morning.

*(HERAK turns his wheel chair and moves away from VLACO. VLACO stares at him a beat. Then VLACO exits. HERAK drops his chin in his hands. Lights fade. Sound punctuates.)*

**VLACO.** *(Addressing the audience. As lights slowly come up on SAMIRA and AMINA in a freeze standing in the exercise yard.)* The rules of the camp were clear. The rules of the camp were strict. All the women here knew the rules of the camp. They all knew how dangerous it was to break the rules, but some did…

*(A shot rings out and quickens SAMIRA and AMINA.)*

**AMINA.** Oh, my. God!

**SAMIRA.** What is it?! *(We hear a scream off.)* It's Jela!

*(JELA enters crying.)*

**AMINA.** Jela…

**SAMIRA.** What happened? Can you speak?

**AMINA.** In the name of Allah. tell us.

**JELA.** Nadia…Nadia…

**JELA AND FEMALE CHORUS.** They killed her! Shot her! Nadia!

**SAMIRA.** No.

**JELA.** One of the truck drivers…turned her in to the guard.

**AMINA.** Turned her in for what?

**VLACO.** *(entering the scene)* For trying to smuggle out information.

**SAMIRA.** Information? What information could she have? That the bread is stale? That the showers are a trickle of cold water?

**VLACO.** You all know the regulations here. It is criminal to...

**JELA.** You're the damned criminal! This is an atrocity! A war crime!

(**AMINA** *pulls* **JELA** *away from* **VLACO.**)

What will they do with her? I want to bury her.

**JELA AND FEMALE CHORUS.** I want to pray over her

**JELA.** before those

**JELA AND FEMALE CHORUS.** bastards

**JELA.** throw her in a

**JELA AND FEMALE CHORUS.** hole like a dead dog.

**AMINA AND FEMALE CHORUS.** Let us all pray for her.

**VLACO.** Only one of you! Only one! This is not a state funeral! One!

**JELA.** Then let me go to her.

**VLACO.** You go ahead then.

(**JELA** *exits. Pause. Then* **AMINA** *and* **SAMIRA** *turn away from* **VLACO.**)

Don't go away. I have an assignment for your daughter.

**SAMIRA.** Me? An assignment.

**AMINA.** What is it now? You're not going to separate us? She's not well.

**VLACO.** The Colonel. He wants your daughter to...to work as his housekeeper.

(*Pause.* **AMINA** *looks relieved, even smiles slightly.*)

**SAMIRA.** Housekeeper?

**VLACO.** In the cabin. Yes. Housekeeper.

**SAMIRA AND FEMALE CHORUS.** Housekeeper

**SAMIRA.** to him?

**VLACO.** A guard will come in the morning.
He'll give you a clean smock.
At night you'll be taken back to your cell.

**SAMIRA AND FEMALE CHORUS.** I won't do it.

**AMINA.** Samira, you'll be out of this cage all day.

**SAMIRA AND FEMALE CHORUS.** I'd rather rot in that cage.

**AMINA.** You can survive here keeping his house.
There's no principle to stand on in a nightmare.
You just want to wake up safe.

**SAMIRA AND FEMALE CHORUS.** They just killed Nadia.

**FEMALE CHORUS.** The smoke from the gun hasn't cleared the camp yet.

**SAMIRA.** And you want me to work in his house?

**VLACO AND MALE CHORUS.** This is not

**VLACO.** a mother-daughter decision. One of my duties here is to keep Colonel Herak happy, and I plan to do just that. So clean yourself up in the morning and comb your hair and…

*(SAMIRA turns away.)*

**AMINA.** She'll be ready, Lieutenant.

**SAMIRA.** You can drag me across this yard to that cabin,

**SAMIRA AND FEMALE CHORUS.** but I won't work. I won't keep house for a man like that.

*(VLACO pushes AMINA out of his way and knocks her down. He moves behind SAMIRA.)*

**VLACO.** You have no choice here. You'll work. You'll do whatever Herak asks – listen carefully…You'll be his housekeeper or your mother will become house-keeper

**VLACO AND MALE CHORUS.** in the guards barracks! Do you understand what I'm saying?

*(SAMIRA turns and nods at him. She looks at her mother on the ground.)*

**VLACO.** Yes. Yes, I can see that you understand perfectly now.

*(Lights fade on the three, Music punctuates.)*

### N.B. If an intermission is desired, this is the end of Act 1

*(As the lights come up slowly on* **HERAK**'s *cabin)*

**VLACO.** *(addressing the audience)* I thought – we all thought – that our Colonel had his eye on the prettiest enemy in the camp. The men who wanted her cursed him for taking her out of their reach. But Herak needed no ordinary barrack's curse. The war, which had been as clear to him as a sailor's star up until now, cursed him with a riddle that squirmed in his brain for an answer: how could this Samira Jusic be his own flesh and blood and yet the enemy?

*(***SAMIRA** *enters* **HERAK**'s *cabin dressed in a white smock. For the first time her hair is combed out. She stands motionless. After a beat,* **HERAK** *sees her.)*

**HERAK.** Oh...yes...Samira Jusic...you...you look tired.

*(***SAMIRA** *doesn't answer.)*

Aren't you sleeping?

**SAMIRA.** I can't sleep. I can't sleep in this place.

**HERAK.** You have to sleep. That's how we recover from one day to the next...anyway, let me tell you where everything is.

**SAMIRA.** Why do you want me here?

**HERAK.** Just some light housekeeping. There's a kitchen in there. This morning some coffee. I like it thick and black and hot. *(pause)* Is something wrong? Didn't Lieutenant Vlaco explain why you were sent here?

**SAMIRA.** Out of all these women, why...

**SAMIRA AND FEMALE CHORUS.** why'd you ask for me? *(pause)*

**SAMIRA.** Well? *(pause)* Because you bought milk from my grandfather a hundred years ago? Or is this the Colonel's genteel way to

**SAMIRA AND FEMALE CHORUS.** rape a woman.

**HERAK.** What makes you think that of me?

**SAMIRA.** It goes on all the time here.

**SAMIRA AND FEMALE CHORUS.** Rape

**SAMIRA.** and the

**SAMIRA AND FEMALE CHORUS.** threat of rape.

**HERAK.** But you haven't been…He threatened you?

**SAMIRA.** You don't think I volunteered to come here to make you the

**SAMIRA AND FEMALE CHORUS.** killer of my people –

**SAMIRA.** some coffee.

**HERAK.** Your…your mother asked me to take you on as a housekeeper.

**SAMIRA.** She asked?

**HERAK.** Yes. To keep you away from…from everything. In Belgrade I have three daughters. I understand. I would never…I mean to say you'll be safe here.

**SAMIRA.** How safe can I be with a

**SAMRIA AND FEMALE CHORUS.** slaughterer like you?

**HERAK AND MALE CHORUS.** I'm a soldier.

**SAMIRA.** That girl they shot – Nadia – was 19.

**HERAK.** In a camp like this…

**SAMIRA AND FEMALE CHORUS.** A prison.

**HERAK.** In a

**HERAK AND MALE CHORUS.** Prison

**HERAK.** like this, it's a capital crime to give information to the enemy.

**HERAK AND MALE CHORUS.** Yes, it's a prison,

**HERAK.** not a girl's school. That girl knew the chance she took. The message she tried to smuggle out was the fact that I'm here in this camp and which building I'm in. She was a danger.

**HERAK AND MALE CHORUS.** There are terrorists out there…

**SAMIRA AND FEMALE CHORUS.** Freedom fighters.

**HERAK AND MALE CHORUS.** Terrorists

**HERAK.** who'd like to have that information.

**SAMIRA.** And your conscience is not bothered that a teen-aged girl was shot through the skull?

**HERAK.** She was warned when she came here. You all were. The enemy comes in any gender, any age. In Goradze, where I took shrapnel, high school boys fired the mortar rounds. We returned fire. It's our duty. We're soldiers.

**SAMIRA.** My father and brother fought in Goradze.

**HERAK AND MALE CHORUS.** They might have fired on my men.

**SAMIRA AND FEMALE CHORUS.** And your return fire might have killed them. *(Pause. They regard each other.)*

**SAMIRA.** But here I am now, going into your kitchen to make your coffee. Thick and black and hot.

**SAMIRA AND FEMALE CHORUS.** Just the way you like it.

> *(**SAMIRA** exits. **HERAK** sits in his chair and stares at her as the lights fade. Music punctuates.)*

> *(as lights slowly come up on **AMINA** and **SAMIRA**)*

**VLACO.** *(addressing the audience)* Now you see Herak's riddle. The dynamic of war is this: the enemy is not just another human being; the enemy is flawed; the enemy is a

**VLACO AND MALE CHORUS.** fascist Croat

**VLACO.** or a

**VLACO AND MALE CHORUS.** Great Satan

**VLACO.** or an

**VLACO AND MALE CHORUS.** Arab infidel,

**VLACO.** and if the enemy's flawed presence in this world is an

**VLACO AND MALE CHORUS.** absolute evil;

**VLACO.** and your presence here is an

**VLACO AND MALE CHORUS.** absolute good;

**VLACO.** then you have no choice but to

**VLACO AND MALE CHORUS.** kill him,

**VLACO.** as if he were a snake at a baby's throat.

> *(**AMINA** and **SAMIRA** quicken.)*

**AMINA.** And so you made coffee

**SAMIRA.** Yes. mother, yes. And he sat there and drank, the whole pot. Why must you have every detail? For lunch I cooked him eggs. Then he went out with Vlaco.

**AMINA.** It's a soft cushion being, up there.

**SAMIRA.** It'd be a softer cushion if they'd let us go.

**AMINA.** Just don't say anything to anger him.

**SAMIRA.** *(laughs)* I said everything I could to anger him. I hate him. He was in Goradze. He probably killed Father and Vedran.

**AMINA AND FEMALE CHORUS.** Don't say that!

**AMINA.** We don't know that they're dead. They'll turn up. I know it. I asked Herak to try to find out about them.

**SAMIRA.** And he said he would?

**AMINA.** He said he would.

**SAMIRA.** Why do you trust him? Why'd you beg him to take me on up there? Why are you so sure he's not worse than any other pig in here? He stared at me the whole while he was in the cabin. He's creepy.

*(JELA enters with plastic bottles of water.)*

**JELA.** Here's your water.

**AMINA.** How are you, Jela?

**JELA.** How can I be? I mean. I buried her. They let me pray over her. The guards tried to stop me. Herak told them to let me pray.

**SAMIRA.** Here. *(She hands JELA some cheese.)* Take it. You need it to keep up your strength.

**JELA.** Cheese? Fresh cheese?

**AMINA.** Herak gave it to her.

**JELA.** Fresh cheese.

**SAMIRA.** He made me take it with me. I won't eat his cheese.

**JELA.** We heard. We heard he took you in to work in his place. You could be valuable to everybody.

**SAMIRA.** How so?

**JELA.** How so? You're in his quarters. When his wounds heal up he'll be sent somewhere and let fire another shit storm on our towns and villages. It would help if we knew where he's going after here. Any information you dig, up, I'll get out.

**AMINA.** Jela, she's not getting into this.

**SAMIRA.** Why're you risking your life getting trivial information out of here"

**JELA.** Trivial?

**JELA AND FEMALE CHORUS.** Trivial!

**JELA.** We have the Great Herak here, and I'll get that out. I'll pick up where poor Nadia left off...

**SAMIRA.** How do you get information out of here?

**JELA.** Truck drivers. They haul out garbage and deliver supplies. Truck drivers.

**SAMIRA.** Why do they take out messages?

**JELA.** You pay them.

**SAMIRA.** Pay them? Pay them with what?

**JELA.** With what? With

**JELA AND FEMALE CHORUS.** your mouth, your tongue,

**JELA.** anything they want...Don't look at me that way.

**JELA AND FEMALE CHORUS.** What else does a woman have here to pay with? God understands

**JELA.** it's in the service of our people...

**AMINA.** We're not getting involved in spying. She's just up there to do the housework.

**JELA.** And she was just at the fuel depot to get a tank of gas.

**SAMIRA.** I would not have done that if I'd known there were people inside.

**JELA.** They weren't people. They were

**JELA AND FEMALE CHORUS.** Serbs. Serb soldiers.

**JELA.** Don't want to be involved. The day and hour the Serbs invaded,

**JELA AND FEMALE CHORUS.** you were involved,

**JELA.** Amina. When your husband and son took up arms.

**JELA AND FEMALE CHORUS.** you were involved.

**JELA.** When your village emptied of men.

**JELA AND FEMALE CHORUS.** you were involved.

**JELA.** Every time you shed a tear, you're Involved. And when the fuel depot went up, your daughter promoted herself to a

**JELA AND FEMALE CHORUS.** defender of Islam.

**JELA.** We're all involved. Look around.

**JELA AND FEMALE CHORUS.** Think where you are.

SAMIRA. All night. All right, Jela…if I hear anything that might be important, I'll pass it on to you. All right?

AMINA AND FEMALE CHORUS. Samira…

SAMIRA. I can at least do that.

JELA. In memory of poor Nadia, Amina. Amina, Samira knows. She knows that even in here, under the thumb of the enemy, we can still fight them. A great battle can go on even in a cesspool like this camp. We keep our dignity when we fight them. They can't rape a woman's

JELA AND FEMALE CHORUS. soul, Amina. It goes pure to Allah.

*(Lights fade. Sound punctuates.)*

*(Lights slowly come up on* HERAK *looking at maps. The wheelchair is now folded up in the back-ground.)*

VLACO. *(addressing the audience)* Now Samira saw a purpose in cooking food and cleaning the Colonel's quarters. Over the weeks she became almost civil to him, trying to induce him to talk about everything. And he…he marveled at how bright she was. Almost every day they had a debate about one thing or another…

*(*SAMIRA *enters with his coffee mug.)*

HERAK. Oh…Thank you…*(He hands her the maps.)* You can put this over there…There are no markings on them.

SAMIRA. What?

HERAK. On the maps. There are no marks on them. You won't find my military strategy scribbled on them. I saw you looking at them yesterday.

SAMIRA. Only to count all the towns your army's stolen.

HERAK. An army doesn't steal.

HERAK AND MALE CHORUS. It conquers.

SAMIRA. Words. You're a teacher. You know how to play with words. The truth is you stole our land.

HERAK. What kind of history do they teach in these schools? This land is Serbian land. The Muslims overran it.

SAMIRA AND FEMALE CHORUS. They conquered it. You overran it.

HERAK AND MALE CHORUS. It was Serb land. We settled it.

SAMIRA. That's ancient history.

**HERAK.** Medieval, actually. Sultan Murod I took our lands by the sword of Islam. 1389.

**SAMIRA.** But our whole culture has grown up here since 1389. If we were Christians, you would not have fired a shot. But because

**SAMIRA AND FEMALE CHORUS.** we're Muslims,

**SAMIRA.** you want it

**SAMIRA AND FEMALE CHORUS.** cleared of the infidels.

**HERAK.** I've never called your people infidels.

**SAMIRA.** But we are to you.

**HERAK.** I'm a Christian. You're a non-Christian.

**SAMIRA AND FEMALE CHORUS.** Non. Nothing. Nobody.

**SAMIRA.** What a polite way to dismiss us. What... – what would you think If one of your daughters loved a Muslim boy?

**HERAK.** I...I would...I would discourage such a relationship.

**SAMIRA.** Why?

**HERAK.** Because...because a Muslim is of another faith, one in which my daughters don't believe. There are differences in the world. Like it or not, there are differences between people.

**SAMIRA.** Yes. Some are good and some are bad.

**HERAK.** No. Not only good and bad. There are differences, Samira. To my daughters,

**HERAK AND MALE CHORUS.** Jesus Christ

**HERAK.** is the center of their whole lives.

**HERAK AND MALE CHORUS.** The center of my life and my wife's life.

**HERAK.** Now why would a Muslim boy want to enter a world he doesn't accept.

**SAMIRA.** But you don't answer my question. What would you do if one of your daughters fell in love with a Muslim boy?

**HERAK.** I said I'd discourage it.

**SAMIRA.** She already loves him and she ignores you.

**SAMIRA AND FEMALE CHORUS.** Suppose

SAMIRA. she ignored you and ran off. It happens.

SAMIRA AND FEMALE CHORUS. Suppose…

SAMIRA. suppose she got pregnant, had a child with that boy?

SAMIRA AND FEMALE CHORUS. Suppose

SAMIRA. your grandson were half a Muslim?
Just suppose.
What would you do if you caught up with them?

SAMIRA AND FEMALE CHORUS. Would you kill them?

SAMIRA. Would you love them? How would you feel about the baby? *(A beat.* HERAK *doesn't answer.)* you can't answer….?

HERAK. It's all suppositions. Samira.

HERAK AND MALE CHORUS. My daughters are devout.

HERAK. Stop supposing and look at life. Your father would never let you see a Christian boy,

HERAK AND MALE CHORUS. a Serbian Christian boy.

SAMIRA. True. That's true. He'd kill me.

SAMIRA AND FEMALE CHORUS. He'd kill both of us.

HERAK. So…so……see how there are differences other than just good and bad? You don't consider your father bad just because he wants you with your own kind. Because his dreams for you would be to marry a Muslim boy. Have you got a boyfriend?

SAMIRA. Boyfriend?

SAMIRA AND FEMALE CHORUS. Where would any Muslim girl find a boyfriend?

SAMIRA. These women you cage up here are missing husbands, brothers, nephews. uncles, neighbors. All gone,

SAMIRA AND FEMALE CHORUS. all gone.

SAMIRA. They all ran off when I was still in school. They ran off before they could be taken by your army. Look in the town. No boys. Just women, children and old men. Old men too far gone to do anything, but puff on their pipes. No. I have no boyfriend, Colonel.

HERAK. I know it's horrible to have families split up like this.

SAMIRA. When you leave here will you go home to see your wife and daughters? Or will you go somewhere else?

**HERAK** *(smiles)* Where I go when I leave here is classified information.

**SAMIRA.** That's right. It would be…in your case…since you're to be made general…They'll be some big time battle for you to plan…you couldn't say…

**SAMIRA AND FEMALE CHORUS.** Do your daughters love you?

**SAMIRA.** I mean to say, you're a career officer. Do they know you well enough to miss you?

**HERAK.** I think they love me and miss me. I'm very good to them.

**HERAK AND MALE CHORUS.** I love them.

**HERAK.** I'd do anything for my daughters.

**HERAK AND MALE CHORUS.** I love them all.

**SAMIRA.** *(after a pause)* Belgrade.

**HERAK.** Belgrade?

**SAMIRA AND FEMALE CHORUS.** They're in Belgrade you said.

**SAMIRA.** You wouldn't take another assignment until you saw them again. You'll go to Belgrade after here.

*(Pause.* **HERAK** *regards her. He smiles.)*

I can see it in your eyes. You do love all your daughters. Oh, don't deny it. You'll go from here to there.

**HERAK AND MALE CHORUS.** You're just like Irena. My oldest daughter and…and…

**SAMIRA.** What is it?

**SAMIRA AND FEMALE CHORUS.** What's Irena like?

**SAMIRA.** Why am I like she?

**HERAK.** Irena…She…She's a pryer. She prys at a person until she finds out what she wants. She…she twists our conversations like taffy, this way and that, until she finds out exactly what I didn't want to tell her.

**MALE CHORUS.** Irena

**HERAK.** Irena.

**SAMIRA.** And she's your favorite. I can tell. Your face…when you mentioned her name…your face…it stopped looking like a soldier's face and it looked like a…like a father's face…

**HERAK.** I always tell them I don't have a favorite.

**SAMIRA.** You don't have to lie to me.

**HERAK.** I could never tell anyone in my family but...

**SAMIRA.** But what?

**HERAK.** Yes. I was just going, to say, yes, Irena is my favorite.

**SAMIRA.** *(taking his empty coffee cup)* I'm sure the others know.

**SAMIRA AND FEMALE CHORUS.** The other's always know...

**SAMIRA.** Belgrade...

> *(***SAMIRA** *exits.* **HERAK** *sits on a riser. He smiles to himself. Lights fade. Sound punctuates.)*

**FEMALE CHORUS.** *(echo)* Belgrade...

**SAMIRA.** Belgrade...

> *(as lights slowly come up on* **AMINA** *and* **SAMIRA** *in their cell)*

**VLACO.** *(addressing the audience)* To perceive this as good and that as evil is a satisfying way to look at the world.

**VLACO AND MALE CHORUS.** Good

**VLACO.** and

**VLACO AND MALE CHORUS.** Evil.

A single vision etched in clarity. A solid moral ruler to measure human action, to order human thought.

**VLACO AND MALE CHORUS.** Good

**VLACO.** and

**VLACO AND MALE CHORUS.** Evil.

**VLACO.** That this measure is often too simple does not diminish its appeal in our lives...when Samira Jusic began to see past the hated uniform that Colonel Herak wore, it disturbed her greatly that she glimpsed a human being.

> *(***SAMIRA** *and* **AMINA** *quicken.)*

**SAMIRA.** It was easier before...it was easier before I got to know him. It was easier when he was just the other side.

AMINA. Oh? And now what is he?

SAMIRA. I don't know. He's somebody's father. He's much like my own father: middle aged, strong in his religious convictions, doting on his children, and he eats as many fried eggs as my own father.

AMINA. And toward you. I mean, after all this time, does he...does he like you?

SAMIRA. Why should he like me? He knows I wish he loses this war, or even that he loses his life.

AMINA AND FEMALE CHORUS. You do?

SAMIRA. Don't you?

SAMIRA AND FEMALE CHORUS. Don't we all?

SAMIRA. Don't we

SAMIRA AND FEMALE CHORUS. wish them all dead?

SAMIRA. I mean, he has a

SAMIRA AND FEMALE CHORUS. family

SAMIRA. and it'd be unfortunate for them. For his

SAMIRA AND FEMALE CHORUS. daughters. His eldest. Irena,

SAMIRA. the one he's closest to. He told me all about her. She'd never get over it. But...but he' s a soldier. And it's a

SAMIRA AND FEMALE CHORUS. soldiers job to die, isn't it?

AMINA. The tone of your voice...

SAMIRA. What?

AMINA. The tone of your voice when you speak of him lately is sad or something.

SAMIRA. He's just not what I expected him to be. He's never mistreated me. I have to watch myself mother... In a place like this, you become so starved for a crumb of humanity that when you get a crumb...it looks like a whole loaf.

AMINA. But we're going to pull through this because of him.

SAMIRA AND FEMALE CHORUS. He's still the other side.

FEMALE CHORUS. Branislav Herak...

**AMINA.** Branislav Herak is…

**SAMIRA.** What?

**AMINA.** My hopes and prayers are that you and me and your father and brother will be together again.

**SAMIRA.** I miss them so much. Vedran looked like a boy in that uniform, as if he were dressing up in his father's clothes. He should be in his shorts out kicking a soccer ball. Now he's got a rifle instead, and

**SAMIRA AND FEMALE CHORUS.** the world has made him a killer.

**SAMIRA.** I can't imagine Vedran or father killing anyone.

**AMINA.** I'm sure Branislav Herak's children can't imagine their father killing anyone.

**SAMIRA.** Do you think Father or Vedran would…would rape a Serbian woman.

**AMINA AND FEMALE CHORUS.** Samira…

**SAMIRA.** I mean, I hear that all sides do it.

**AMINA.** When your father and brother left our house they never degraded any human being.

**SAMIRA.** But when they left our house, they left for war, Mother. I think war twists the face of humanity, I do, wrings out the decency…That's why everyone now is

**SAMIRA AND FEMALE CHORUS.** in some way a monster…

**AMINA AND FEMALE CHORUS.** We're not monsters.

**AMINA.** No one in our family is a…

**SAMIRA.** I

**SAMIRA AND FEMALE CHORUS.** burned 16 soldiers to death.

**AMINA.** Shhh…

**SAMIRA.** Me. Samira. who used to go to school with red ribbons in her hair, who couldn't sleep at night unless the cat was in bed with her. I burned 16 people to death. I thought I'd never sleep again when I found out. I thought these lids would stay open forever. It's scary, Mother. Now, only a few weeks later…I sleep.

**SAMIRA AND FEMALE CHORUS.** I sleep soundly.

**SAMIRA.** I sleep on this cement floor as if it were grandmother's big fluffy mattress. Only, when the guard pounds on this cage in the morning, do I wake up. It's scary.

**SAMIRA AND FEMALE CHORUS.** It's scary that we can get over killing people.

**SAMIRA.** It's scary, Mother...

*(Lights fade. Music punctuates.)*

*(as lights come up slowly on a freeze of* **HERAK** *lighting a cigarette)*

**VLACO.** *(addressing the audience)* I always assumed that a man of Herak's fame knew what he was doing. That he calculated everything, designed before he decided, engineered before he acted. Hence his brilliance in winning battles. But this thing with the Jusic girl, a prisoner, seemed to me an aberration, a lapse in judgment, an error. Sweetcakes. Good Christ, I said.

**VLACO AND MALE CHORUS.** Sweetcakes!

*(***HERAK*** looks through papers and documents.* **SAMIRA** *enters with a tray of food.)*

**SAMIRA.** Where'd you get all this? I haven't seen beef this good in years.

**HERAK.** Eat some if you like. *(***HERAK*** sits and eats.)*

**SAMIRA.** I did already...I tasted some.

**HERAK.** You should have something good today yes, I know today's a special day for you.

*(Pause.* **SAMIRA** *looks at him.)*

**SAMIRA.** She told You. My mother told you.

**HERAK.** No. Your birth date is on your identification papers. Twenty years old today.

**SAMIRA.** Twenty, years old.

**HERAK.** A child no longer

**SAMIRA.** I haven't been a child since...

**SAMIRA AND FEMALE CHORUS.** Since death wiped the innocence from my eyes.

SAMIRA. I remember the day…coming home from school…
they were right in front of me…a man and his wife
crossing, the street…a sniper's bullet struck him. The
crowd ran…the man's blood splattered his wife…a
whole cloudburst of blood…He fell…

SAMIRA AND FEMALE CHORUS. Shock froze me.

SAMIRA. I didn't hear the others shouting at me to get
down. Someone grabbed at my collar and yanked me
into a doorway, but I could still see the wife screaming
and holding her hand over the wound, as if her little
trembling white hand could stop the giant death that
tore up her husband's heart…I never even told my
mother I was so close to them when he was hit…

HERAK. I know the shock and numbness you speak of…
Believe me. Believe me when I tell you, I pray, I pray
the politicians go to the blessed peace table every day.

HERAK AND MALE CHORUS. Believe me, I pray for peace.

HERAK. Look…Samira…may we suspend the war for three
minutes so I can give you this. *(He hands her a white
box.)*

SAMIRA. What's this?

HERAK. I don't know. It's a…a birthday present.

SAMIRA. A birthday…in this place?.. a present? *(She opens
the box.)*

SAMIRA AND FEMALE CHORUS. Sweetcakes?

SAMIRA. Sweetcakes.

SAMIRA AND FEMALE CHORUS. How'd you ever get sweetcakes?

HERAK. We have supply routes. No, I won't tell you which
roads we use. Eat.

SAMIRA. *(tasting the cakes)* They're fresh. They're good…
Thank you…

HERAK. You're welcome.

SAMIRA. You're leaving here soon. Aren't you?

HERAK. Well, I'm feeling better now and…

SAMIRA. And so you go again to fight…

**SAMIRA AND FEMALE CHORUS.** the war...*(She puts the cake down.)*

**SAMIRA.** The sweet taste...

**SAMIRA AND FEMALE CHORUS.** it almost made me forget.

**HERAK** *(rising)* Think what you will of me. But remember this. I don't relish war. My country called on me and I answered. I was a teacher, Samira. I taught all the old wars as if they were all just a long ago history. Then when this business started in our country, I couldn't believe that the people wanted war. They all planned for it. They paid for it. Unfurled flags in wars' honor. Cheered for it as if it were a national sporting event. And now we die for it. And children swallow their childhood before their time. I don't want you to think I'm in this to become a General or a hero. I gamble everything I love in this fight.

**HERAK AND MALE CHORUS.** My home. My wife...my daughters.

**SAMIRA.** Why do you care what I think?

**HERAK.** A young girl...Samira...has got to know more than hate. I can see it's consuming you, destroying you.

*(VLACO enters with mail.)*

**VLACO.** Colonel...

**HERAK.** Yes, Lieutenant.

**VLACO.** Daily dispatches, Sir.

*(HERAK takes the dispatches and signals SAMIRA to remove the food tray.)*

**HERAK.** And Samira. you take these sweetcakes back with you tonight. They go stale fast.

**SAMIRA.** Yes...yes...thank you

*(SAMIRA removes the food tray and exits. VLACO looks inside the box. HERAK sits and reads.)*

**VLACO.** Sweetcakes.

**VLACO AND MALE CHORUS.** Good Christ. Sweetcakes!

**HERAK.** What's the matter?

**VLACO.** I just remarked on the sweetcakes. Sir.

**HERAK.** Yes. The girl's birthday…she's twenty years old now and she still has a child's face. Don't you think she deserves…

*(He stops abruptly at his reading of one of the dispatches and rises.)*

**VLACO.** She might have a child's face, but she's got a killers brain.

**HERAK.** *(far away in thought for a moment)* Some of the men would shoot them all, line them up and shoot them all, wouldn't they? All these women?

**VLACO.** Some of them only need the order, Sir. But I…

**HERAK.** But you…you're not one of them, are you, Lieutenant? You just begrudge a girl a few sweetcakes on her birthday.

**VLACO.** I remarked on you giving her sweetcakes, because I have news, Sir. I don't give a damn if it's the girl's birthday or not. Three of the women have been broken down and made to spill their insides.

**HERAK.** And…

**VLACO.** And, Sir, the three give separate detailed corroborating accounts of how this birthday girl with the child's face and the sweetcakes on her breath…

**HERAK.** Lieutenant

**VLACO.** Blew up the fuel depot, Sir.

**HERAK.** Her? Samira Jusic.

**HERAK AND MALE CHORUS.** They name her?

**VLACO.** Samira Jusic drove the Citroen packed with the explosives that did the deed.

*(long pause)*

Sir?

**HERAK.** What did we do to those women to, as you say, break them down?

**VLACO.** We were firm but not brutal.

*(**HERAK** laughs.)*

**HERAK.** We play with words, Samira once told me.

**HERAK AND MALE CHORUS.** Firm but not brutal.

**HERAK.** What does that mean? You only put your rifle

**HERAK AND MALE CHORUS.** half way up their asses,

**HERAK.** not all the way?

**VLACO.** Sir, I don't understand. I thought you'd be pleased to know. How...how do you want to...to proceed?

**HERAK.** Don't shoot her right now, Lieutenant.
     She's not finished washing the dishes out there.

**VLACO.** Colonel Herak, what is it? I'm only asking what you want me to do?

**HERAK.** Yes. Yes. I know. Well, she's here in the kitchen... we've got her...she's not going any place...I'll...I'll decide what's to be done.

**VLACO.** Maybe if you read the signed statements of these women...

**HERAK.** Yes...yes, leave them...leave them and go.

*(Pause. **VLACO** does not move.)*

     Well?

**VLACO.** You seem angry, Sir. Oh, I understand the girl kept your quarters clean and that...that you got to know her...

**HERAK.** What does that mean?

**HERAK AND MALE CHORUS.** I got to know her.

**HERAK.** Lieutenant, do the men think that I...that this girl and I

**VLACO.** Sir, what do you expect the men to think? She's pretty and you...quite frankly, Sir...you seem to...to favor her...

**HERAK.** Jovan Vlaco, you can inform the men that what they think isn't true. That what they think is through the squalor of their own war weary minds.

**VLACO.** Yes, Sir.

**HERAK.** And if she did destroy the fuel depot, it's because she became a soldier for her people, just as we have for our people.

**VLACO AND MALE CHORUS.** She killed 16 soldiers.

**VLACO.** Sir.

(*HERAK hands* **VLACO** *the dispatch he had been reading.*)

**HERAK.** And we fucking killed her father and her brother!

**VLACO.** (*looking at the dispatch*) Shot. Shot trying to escape…

(**SAMIRA** *enters with Herak's coffee. They both turn to look at her. Lights fade. Music punctuates.*)

(*addressing the audience*) I couldn't understand at the time why Herak cared if two enemy soldiers were shot escaping. It happened daily all over. I couldn't understand at the time why he didn't shoot this Samira himself now that we had proof against her…

(*Lights come up slowly on* **AMINA** *in the camp yard. They comfort each other.*)

What was wrong with him? Battle fatigue? Had he lost his nerve for what has to be done in war?

I was blind to what he thought. To me, Samira Jusic was a saboteur for the Bosnian army. And so should she be to Herak…

(**AMINA** *and* **SAMIRA** *begin crying. After a beat,* **JELA** *enters and crosses to them.*)

**JELA.** I heard…I'm sorry for you both…I'm sorry…

**AMINA.** He was a boy…Vedran was a boy, Jela…He drank milk from the carton…He threw his clothes on the floor…He kicked his soccer ball in the yard…He loved soccer as only a boy can…

**AMINA AND FEMALE CHORUS.** They killed a boy. They killed a boy and his father!

**JELA.** The whole camp mourns with you. Your son and your husband are heroes.

**AMINA.** They're dead! Calling them heroes doesn't draw out the sting! They're dead!

(**AMINA** *falls to her knees crying.* **JELA** *puts her arm around* **SAMIRA** *and takes her aside.* **AMINA**'s *sobs punctuate the exchange between* **JELA** *and* **SAMIRA**.)

**JELA.** Can you pull yourself together and listen to me? I don't have a lot of time. They saw me. They saw.

**SAMIRA.** Who?

**JELA.** Listen. I have a message for you from the leader of your group. They know you work in Herak's place.

**SAMIRA.** But I refuse to go back there.

**JELA.** You have to. You told us he'd be leaving, soon.

**SAMIRA.** Who cares? Who cares about any of it now? Passing your information back and forth. Who cares?

**SAMIRA AND FEMALE CHORUS.** My family's been butchered'

**JELA.** Then maybe this is the best time to act.

**SAMIRA.** On what?

**JELA AND FEMALE CHORUS.** They don't want Herak to leave here.

**JELA.** They don't want him back in the war. They want him killed, Samira.

**SAMIRA AND FEMALE CHORUS.** Killed?

**AMINA.** *(to herself)* Such a good father was he...such a good husband...

**SAMIRA.** They want me...

**JELA.** *(handing her a small vial)* You take it. Take it. There's not much time. They saw me. Samira. They saw them pass this to me...

**SAMIRA.** What...what is it?

**JELA.** In strong coffee. He won't taste it.

**SAMIRA.** Jela...Jela...I...I can't do this...I never

**SAMIRA AND FEMALE CHORUS.** killed anyone.

**JELA.** You

**JELA AND FEMALE CHORUS.** killed 16.

**FEMALE CHORUS.** I can't.

**SAMIRA.** I can't.

**JELA.** It's your group leader who orders this.

*(She presses **SAMIRA**'s hand.)*

It's from them.

**SAMIRA AND FEMALE CHORUS.** I can't.

JELA. Don't look at me like that. Don't say you can't. You can't. Why not? You forgot the war? Up in that cabin every day, eating the best foods. Drinking good coffee. Listening to his sweet nothings in your ears.

(SAMIRA *grabs* JELA.)

SAMIRA. You fool! Do you use your mouth for anything that's not foul?!

SAMIRA AND FEMALE CHORUS. Stupid, stupid

SAMIRA. little fool!

JELA *(pulling away)* Why a fool?

SAMIRA. It's not true.

JELA. If it's not true then, just kill him. Kill him.

JELA AND FEMALE CHORUS. Kill the bastard.

AMINA. *(again to herself, out of the loop of Jela and Samira)* We'll never see them again ever.

JELA. Why should your father die and he live?

SAMIRA. Look at my mother.

AMINA AND FEMALE CHORUS. Is any water more bitter than a widow's tear?

SAMIRA. Look at her.

FEMALE CHORUS. Where her heart was there is now nothing, but grief.

SAMIRA. I'm all she has left. What do you think they'll do to me when they find this in the great Herak's vomit?

(She holds up the vial.)

JELA. It'll all turn out the same for you. For me too.

SAMIRA. What'll turn out the same?

JELA. Do you want your short life to matter?

SAMIRA. What're you talking about?

JELA. Some of the others. They talked. From your village. They talked. Torture opens mouths. Electricity they use. Electricity does more than burn the Colonel's toast. They know.

JELA AND FEMALE CHORUS. The fuel depot. They know you did it.

**JELA.** So how long do you have? It's only because of Herak that they haven't put out the back of your head. It's only because you and Herak are...because he's using, you...

**SAMIRA.** He's not!

**SAMIRA AND FEMALE CHORUS.** He's not using me!

**SAMIRA.** He's not like that!

**SAMIRA AND FEMALE CHORUS.** He never touched me!

**SAMIRA.** Never once!

**MALE CHORUS MEMBER.** It's that one there, Lieutenant! It's her, The one who takes the bread around! She's the one!

(*VLACO and the soldier enter.* **AMINA** *crosses to* **SAMIRA** *and* JELA.)

**AMINA.** What is it now?

(*VLACO slowly crosses to* **JELA**. *He takes her arm and bends it back behind her.*)

**JELA.** What? What is it?

**SAMIRA.** Leave her alone!

**VLACO.** We know you received something through the fence. They saw you take it and run.

**VLACO AND MALE CHORUS.** What did they give you?

**JELA.** Nothing. I have nothing. Nothing. Search me.

**VLACO.** You were seen taking something.

**JELA.** I have nothing!

**VLACO.** Maybe you swallowed it just now!

**VLACO AND MALE CHORUS.** Maybe we'll have to hose it out of you!

(JELA *screams off.* **AMINA** *resumes crying.* **SAMIRA** *holds her mother and looks at the vial in her hand. Lights fade. Music punctuates.*)

**VLACO.** (*addressing the audience*) Jela Kaljanao was one of the strongest women I've ever encountered. Under torture she revealed nothing. She just cursed the guards through her electric pain.

**FEMALE CHORUS AND JELA.** God is great! Soon. Soon I'll be dead, you bastards! God is great! Soon, I'll see God and I'll know why he sent you bastards here! Yes, I'll know. I'LL KNOW WHY HE SENT THIS WAR! AND YOU'LL STILL BE IN THIS DARKNESS, THIS SUFFERING…THIS UNBEARABLE SUFFERING!!

**VLACO.** *(addressing the audience)* Jela now knows why God sent this war and we are still in darkness and suffering and the guilt that debilitates us like an illness…

*(HERAK in his cabin. After a beat SAMIRA enters. HERAK sees her. Slowly, he rises.)*

**HERAK.** I…I told them…I told them you didn't have to come back here if you didn't want to…It's al I right. Nothing will happen to you…Samira? Samira, you want some coffee? I made some…I'm…I'm sorry about your father and your brother…

**SAMIRA.** I always knew they were dead. You know that. It was mother who always had hope. It's Jela. We want to bury her.

**SAMIRA AND FEMALE CHORUS.** We want to bury her with prayers

**SAMIRA.** not only dirt.

**HERAK.** Yes. Yes. Look, I said before these women take their lives in their own hands when they go to the forbidden zones near the fences to smuggle contraband in here.

**HERAK AND MALE CHORUS.** The woman knew that.

**SAMIRA.** Woman. She was not much older than I am. Not much older than your oldest daughter.

**HERAK.** My daughter wouldn't have…

**SAMIRA.** If the war were in her backyard, she'd do exactly what we do.

**SAMIRA AND FEMALE CHORUS.** Look at us. We're all somebody's daughter!

**SAMIRA.** Your daughter would do exactly as we do and

**SAMIRA AND FEMALE CHORUS.** hate as savagely as we do.

**HERAK.** And what exactly did you do in this war?

**SAMIRA.** Only…only what I had to do. *(pause)*
Only what the war made me do. *(pause)*
Don't toy with me, please. I know you know about me.
I know. Why? Why am I alive and Jela's dead? Why?

*(pause)*

Why have you shielded me? Jela only passed information in and out. But me…why?

**HERAK.** I…I confess, Samira, that getting to know you over
the weeks, I've grown fond of you…And now I'm at
odds within myself…

**SAMIRA.** So they'll attach their batteries to my breasts after
you leave here.

**HERAK.** I'm

**HERAK AND MALE CHORUS.** trying

**HERAK.** to think of a way of

**HERAK AND MALE CHORUS.** saving you and your mother.

**SAMIRA.** 16 soldiers died in that fuel depot. Your soldiers.
You must be really fond of me. If you're so fond of me,

**SAMIRA AND FEMALE CHORUS.** why didn't you just take me?!

**HERAK.** Samira…

**SAMIRA.** I would've given myself to you to save Jela.

**SAMIRA AND FEMALE CHORUS.** I would not have resisted.

**HERAK.** Stop this.

**SAMIRA.** Did you know that?

**SAMIRA.** You looked surprised. You didn't think I'd be so
quick to give. but to save her, I'd have let you help
yourself.

**HERAK.** You don't know what you're saying!

**HERAK AND MALE CHORUS.** You don't understand!

**HERAK.** I'm…I'm trying…I'm trying to help you because
there have been so many

**HERAK AND MALE CHORUS.** atrocities in this war

**HERAK.** that I…I…I just want to…to

**HERAK AND MALE CHORUS.** help a mother and her daughter to…

**SAMIRA AND FEMALE CHORUS.** No.

**FEMALE CHORUS.** No.

**SAMIRA.** I won't be used for your atonement. You think you're more decent than the others. You want to give us pity now. Pity from a Christian Serb for a Muslim and her mother. The soon to be General Herak who'll go out of this place and kill some more.

**SAMIRA AND FEMALE CHORUS.** You're nothing but a killer

**SAMIRA.** the same as I am! The war's made us into freaks.

**SAMIRA AND FEMALE CHORUS.** Look at us.

**SAMIRA.** If you were decent, you would have done something to save Jela before they…

**HERAK.** Jela Kaljanao

**HERAK AND MALE CHORUS.** chose to be a soldier.

**HERAK.** She chose to fight. Her silence was her rifle. We all fight in different ways with different weapons.

**SAMIRA.** And I chose a car full of explosives. When will they come for me? What happens to me?

**HERAK.** Samira, I'm not going to another detention camp. I can't have you and your mother transferred. But before I leave, I…I can release you both.

**SAMIRA.** It won't do any good.

**HERAK AND MALE CHORUS.** Samira…

**SAMIRA.** They'd just pick us up again after your car is out of sight.

**SAMIRA AND FEMALE CHORUS.** There's no hope. None.

**SAMIRA.** But I want to bury Jela.

**SAMIRA AND FEMALE CHORUS.** We owe the dead a final dignity.

**HERAK.** Of course…of course, you'll be able to bury her… yes…

**SAMIRA.** Thank you. *(She begins to cross off.)*

**HERAK.** Where are you going?

**SAMIRA.** It's time…

**SAMIRA AND JELA.** for your coffee.

**HERAK.** Oh…oh, yes…

**SAMIRA.** *(exiting)* Dark, thick and hot...

**HERAK.** *(alone)* I will find a way...I will...

*(Lights fade. Music punctuates.)*

**VLACO.** *(addressing the audience)* Samira gave him his coffee and left the cabin through the kitchen door. While Herak drank, he put in a call to the United Nations post in Sarajevo. He requested they send a U.N. vehicle to take Amina and Samira Jusic to the safe haven of the Bosnian capitol.

*(Lights come up on* **SAMIRA** *and* **AMINA.**)

I saw Samira leave the cabin. It was unusual to see her leave so early. There was no sign of nervousness or internal calamity. She slowly strolled up to her mother in the yard...

**SAMIRA.** Mother...Mother, stop crying...Mother...

**SAMIRA AND FEMALE CHORUS.** There's not a lot of time...

**SAMIRA.** Mother, they know.

**AMINA.** They know?

**SAMIRA.** About the fuel depot. They know I did it.

**AMINA AND FEMALE CHORUS.** Samira, no. Who said so?

**SAMIRA.** Listen, listen, listen to me. You've got to be stronger now than you've ever been. I don't know, how long it'll be before they come for me. And mother I'm scared.

**AMINA.** Samira...

**SAMIRA.** It's all over for me and that's why I did this. I did it for Father and Vedran.

**AMINA.** Did what? Go to Herak. Go back right now...

**SAMIRA.** Mother! Mother!

**SAMIRA AND FEMALE CHORUS.** Mother! Listen!

**SAMIRA** There's no more Herak.

**AMINA.** What? What're you saying? What did you do?

**SAMIRA.** In his coffee...Just now...In his coffee...

**SAMIRA AND FEMALE CHORUS.** poison...

**SAMIRA.** It was one

**SAMIRA AND FEMALE CHORUS.** last act for God

SAMIRA. that I could perform on this earth. Mother, I love you. Hold me tight.

AMINA. What have you done?! You poisoned Branislav Herak?

SAMIRA. I poisoned Herak the Serb, Mother.

SAMIRA AND FEMALE CHORUS. Herak the Satan, Christian jail keeper, Serb invader, killer, butcher…

AMINA. He's your father!

AMINA AND FEMALE CHORUS. *(as she slaps* SAMIRA*)* Branisiav Herak is your father!

*(*AMINA *starts to run off.* SAMIRA *stops her.)*

SAMIRA. Mother, what is this? Mother!

AMINA. He's your father! Yes!

SAMIRA. My…my…

AMINA. When he was stationed here many years ago…when we were young…He and I…He's your father…Let me go to him.

*(She runs off.)*

SAMIRA. My father…So that's why he…that's why…

*(*SAMIRA *puts her hands to her mouth and cries out. Then she runs after* AMINA. *Black out. Music punctuates.)*

VLACO. *(Addressing the audience as lights slowly come up on* HERAK *bent over holding his stomach. His coffee cup lays on the floor.)*

Amina Jusic bolted across the exercise yard. Samira followed. The other prisoners fell silent. All heads turned like a herd startled at an observed terror in one of their own. I drew my pistol and, at first, tried to stop them from entering…

*(*AMINA, SAMIRA *and* VLACO *enter.)*

Sir…Sir…The Jusic woman claims you're in danger… sir…sir, what is it, Colonel? Colonel!

*(*AMINA *rushes to him.* VLACO *tries to stop her.* HERAK *waves his efforts off.* AMINA *crosses to him and takes his arm and sits him down.)*

**AMINA.** Branislav...Branislav, she didn't know...

(**SAMIRA** *falls to her knees weeping.*)

Maybe a doctor...

**HERAK.** No doctor could stop this...

**VLACO.** Stop what?! What is it, Sir?

**SAMIRA.** He's poisoned. I poisoned him.

**VLACO.** Poisoned?! Sir, let me get a medic and a...

**HERAK.** It won't do any good to get anyone...

**AMINA.** I thought God answered my prayers when he sent you here.

(**VLACO** *crosses to* **SAMIRA** *with a drawn pistol.*)

**HERAK.** No! Don't touch her! Vlaco...don't...

**HERAK AND MALE CHORUS.** don't touch her!

**VLACO.** Why not? I'll shoot this filthy Muslim bitch!

**AMINA.** No!

**SAMIRA AND FEMALE CHORUS.** Shoot! Shoot me! Shoot the life out of me so I won't see any more death!

**HERAK.** No! Put the pistol down!
She's my daughter, Vlaco!

**HERAK AND MALE CHORUS.** She's my daughter!

**VLACO.** Your daughter?

(**SAMIRA** *rises and crosses to* **HERAK,** *her body trembling.*)

**HERAK.** My daughter...my daughter whom this war turned into a soldier...damned good soldier...

**HERAK.** Courage...it took courage...to...to...do this...

(**SAMIRA** *kneels again and cries.*)

**VLACO.** Your daughter...your daughter...

**HERAK.** That I'd never known until now...I grew...grew to love her...
Forbid you to...to touch her...Forbid you...

(**HERAK** *dies and slumps to the floor. Lights dim but do not go down on this tableau. A stark light comes up downstage.* **VLACO** *drops his pistol and races downstage. He seems to choke with pain.*)

**VLACO.** My mouth is dry from the telling. Amina Jusic sobbed out the whole story while I stood there in shock. I did nothing to the two women...I simply walked out of the Colonel's cabin...after that. I deserted the Serbian army...God help me.., I can't sleep anymore... when I witnessed a daughter killing the father – her own father – who was trying to save her...

**FEMALE CHORUS.** Shoot me! Shoot me! Shoot the life out of me, so I won't see anymore death!

**MALE CHORUS.** No! No, Vlaco. She's my daughter!

*(**VLACO** throws off his military jacket.)*

**VLACO.** No more! Please, God. no more!...By the time the U.N. car arrived at the compound to take the two women to a safe city, it was too late. The new commandant had shot both mother and daughter...

*(We hear shots. The light now abruptly blacks out on the tableau and the stark light on **VLACO** begins to fade.)*

I deserted because all I had seen I knew was a sign to me from God almighty...a sign...a sign to stop justifying this...this sin...to stop warping life into death... and saying it is good...to stop...to stop...to stop...to just stop...

*(The lights are out. Music soft up.)*

**The End**

Also by Jules Tasca...

A Medieval Romance

The God's Honest, An Evening of Lies

The Mind with the Dirty Man

Outrageous!

Shylock's Daughter and Other
Small Chips from Great Gems of
Shakespeare

Spirit of Hispania: Hispanic Tales

Subject to Change

Please visit our website **samuelfrench.com** for complete
descriptions and licensing information

# OTHER TITLES AVAILABLE FROM SAMUEL FRENCH

## THREE MUSKETEERS
Ken Ludwig

*All Groups / Adventure / 8m, 4f (doubling) / Unit sets*
This adaptation is based on the timeless swashbuckler by Alexandre Dumas, a tale of heroism, treachery, close escapes and above all, honor. The story, set in 1625, begins with d'Artagnan who sets off for Paris in search of adventure. Along with d'Artagnan goes Sabine, his sister, the quintessential tomboy. Sent with d'Artagnan to attend a convent school in Paris, she poses as a young man – d'Artagnan's servant – and quickly becomes entangled in her brother's adventures. Soon after reaching Paris, d'Artagnan encounters the greatest heroes of the day, Athos, Porthos and Aramis, the famous musketeers; d'Artagnan joins forces with his heroes to defend the honor of the Queen of France. In so doing, he finds himself in opposition to the most dangerous man in Europe, Cardinal Richelieu. Even more deadly is the infamous Countess de Winter, known as Milady, who will stop at nothing to revenge herself on d'Artagnan – and Sabine – for their meddlesome behavior. Little does Milady know that the young girl she scorns, Sabine, will ultimately save the day.

# OTHER TITLES AVAILABLE FROM SAMUEL FRENCH

## GUTENBERG! THE MUSICAL!
### Scott Brown and Anthony King

*Musical Comedy / 2m*

In this two-man musical spoof, a pair of aspiring playwrights perform a backers' audition for their new project - a big, splashy musical about printing press inventor Johann Gutenberg. With an unending supply of enthusiasm, Bud and Doug sing all the songs and play all the parts in their crass historical epic, with the hope that one of the producers in attendance will give them a Broadway contract – fulfilling their ill-advised dreams.

"A smashing success!"
*- The New York Times*

"Brilliantly realized and side-splitting!
*- New York Magazine*

"There are lots of genuine laughs in *Gutenberg!*"
*- The New York Post*

Printed in the United States
154219LV00005B/74/P

9 780573 696268